For Laura and Riley

Richard Molloy

EVERY DAY I MAKE
GREATNESS HAPPEN

OBERON BOOKS
LONDON

WWW.OBERONBOOKS.COM

First published in 2018 by Oberon Books Ltd
521 Caledonian Road, London N7 9RH
Tel: +44 (0) 20 7607 3637 / Fax: +44 (0) 20 7607 3629
e-mail: info@oberonbooks.com
www.oberonbooks.com

A catalogue record for this book is available from the British Library.

PB ISBN: 9781786825926
E ISBN: 9781786825933

Cover image by altmodern

10 9 8 7 6 5 4 3 2 1

Every Day I Make Greatness Happen was first performed at Hampstead Theatre Downstairs, London, on 13 September 2018 with the following cast and creative team:

ALISHA	Sofia Barclay
KAREEM	Moe Bar-El
JOHN	Jon Foster
MISS	Susan Stanley
IMAN	Josh Zaré
Director	Alice Hamilton
Designer	Lucy Sierra
Lighting	Nic Holdridge
Composer and Sound Designer	Ed Lewis

Thank you

Edward Hall, Greg Ripley-Duggan, Amelia Cherry, Will Mortimer, Katharine Noble, Jess Woodward, Lucie Blockley, Chiara Wakely, Pascale Giudicelli, Hilary Williamson, Nick Aldrich, Emily Holmden, Avril Cook, Emily Louise Palmer, Tamsin Rose, Davina Moss, Emlyn Lumley, Teresa Halpin, Megan Hubbard, Salma Hoque, Daniel Rabin, Adam Colbourne, Ashraf Ejjbair, Andrew Keatley, Cathal Cleary, Sarah Goldberg, Carrie Crowley, Mary Meyler, Philip Molloy, Sheila Wayman, Jon Foster, Moe Bar-El, Sofia Barclay, Josh Zaré, Lucy Sierra, Ed Lewis, Nicholas Holdridge, Ciara Dredge, Amy Richardson, Frank and Patricia Byrne.

Special thanks to Alice Hamilton, Susan Stanley, Celia Atkin, and Laura Molloy.

Every Day I Make Greatness Happen was first performed at Hampstead Theatre Downstairs, London, on 13 September 2018 with the following cast and creative team:

ALISHA	Sofia Barclay
KAREEM	Moe Bar-El
JOHN	Jon Foster
MISS	Susan Stanley
IMAN	Josh Zaré
Director	Alice Hamilton
Designer	Lucy Sierra
Lighting	Nic Holdridge
Composer and Sound Designer	Ed Lewis

Thank you

Edward Hall, Greg Ripley-Duggan, Amelia Cherry, Will Mortimer, Katharine Noble, Jess Woodward, Lucie Blockley, Chiara Wakely, Pascale Giudicelli, Hilary Williamson, Nick Aldrich, Emily Holmden, Avril Cook, Emily Louise Palmer, Tamsin Rose, Davina Moss, Emlyn Lumley, Teresa Halpin, Megan Hubbard, Salma Hoque, Daniel Rabin, Adam Colbourne, Ashraf Ejjbair, Andrew Keatley, Cathal Cleary, Sarah Goldberg, Carrie Crowley, Mary Meyler, Philip Molloy, Sheila Wayman, Jon Foster, Moe Bar-El, Sofia Barclay, Josh Zaré, Lucy Sierra, Ed Lewis, Nicholas Holdridge, Ciara Dredge, Amy Richardson, Frank and Patricia Byrne.

Special thanks to Alice Hamilton, Susan Stanley, Celia Atkin, and Laura Molloy.

Characters

MISS, *mid-thirties, Irish*

IMAN, *16, born in London to Iranian parents*

KAREEM, *17, born in London to Egyptian parents*

ALISHA, *17, born in London to Indian parents*

JOHN, *mid-forties, English*

Setting
A classroom in a falling-apart state high school
in London – one of the reviled new Labour/Tory
academies, though not part of an academy chain.

Time
September, 2016 – late January, 2017.

Note
An ellipsis after a character's name indicates
an unwillingness or an inability to speak or, in
some cases, a failure on the character's part to
realise that speaking is expected of him or her.

Act One

September, 2016.

A classroom in a crumbling prefab at a run-down London academy. The students' desks are cheap and shabby – arranged, not in rows, but in clusters of four: squares and L-shapes. The teacher's desk is cluttered – on it, there's a desktop computer, a laptop, a pot of markers, glue-sticks, scissors, a set of exercise books, and a two-tiered plastic tray overflowing with old pieces of paper, worksheets, a disused exercise book or two, and an errant copy of 'Of Mice and Men'. Dog-eared posters and tatty student-made displays, some several years old, adorn the walls. Yellow-brown water stains blossom on the ceiling tiles. A single door leads out into the corridor; a glass panel is fitted into the upper half of the door.

At lights up, the room is empty. A moment passes before MISS enters quietly. She stands still. She looks around, takes everything in – she has been here in this room many, many times before, but somehow this is different. Her entering the room now is a small but momentous feat. She takes a deep breath and…

The lights begin to fade. Sound swells: the life of the school – bustling corridors, screams in the playground, unruly students, the pulse of an electronic bell. All of which carries on into…

Darkness.

And then, at last, a moment of silence.

When the lights come up again, the room is empty once more. We hear a knock on the door. A few seconds later, the door opens tentatively, and IMAN sticks his head in. He looks around then enters. A sixth former, IMAN wears what the school describes as 'smart, business dress' – in his case, chinos or cheap slacks, a shirt and tie, a plain sweater, and a pair of clunky, unfashionable shoes, all of which serves to exacerbate his inherent self-consciousness and social unease. On his back, he carries a massive school bag. For a few seconds, he stands by the door, unsure what to do – he then sits down at one of the desks, opens his bag, takes out a bulging pencil case and an A4 notepad. From the pencil case, he removes a pen and a highlighter. He sets out everything neatly on the desk – he is ready to work.

After a short pause, KAREEM makes a bold, theatrical entrance. He too is a sixth former, but his attire is a little more stylish than IMAN's, and where IMAN is skinny and awkward, KAREEM brims with tall, handsome swagger. He takes a seat somewhere behind IMAN, dumping his bag on the desk. Neither boy makes any acknowledgement of the other.

Silence. KAREEM bristles with barely contained energy. IMAN is visibly, painfully uncomfortable.

Eventually, KAREEM opens his bag and removes a notepad. He then rummages in the bag again, but this time he can't find what he's looking for. He has a thought – he stands up and goes to IMAN's desk. Still without acknowledging the other boy, KAREEM picks up IMAN's pencil case and takes out a pen. He then drops the pencil case very deliberately on the floor, before returning to his desk and retaking his seat. After a pause, IMAN bends over to pick up the pencil case. He waits – considers his next move – then turns around slowly.

IMAN: …Uh…That's not…You can't just…

> *KAREEM double-takes as though he's just noticed for the first time that IMAN is in the room.*

KAREEM: *(A massive fake smile.)* Oh. Hey Iman. How are you?

IMAN: …Uhm…Okay –

KAREEM: Good. Good. Glad to hear it.

> *Short pause.*

KAREEM: Another year, hah…? Another September. Nah, what am I sayin', man? September's almost gone. Time's winged chariot, fam. Gallops apace, innit…Yeah….Bit of Shakespeare for you there. *Romeo and Juliet.* Dunno why I'm here, bruv. I'm sick at English. 'Cept for writin'…And readin'. Books and shit. Fuck that…You like films, innit? *Romeo and Juliet*: that was a sick film. Leonardo da Vinci is a wicked actor. *And* he invented the helicopter…You sure you're okay, Iman? Seem a bit quiet. Somethin' wrong…?

IMAN: …

Defeated, IMAN sighs, bows his head, turns around again.

KAREEM: No…? Well. Great to see you. Thanks for stoppin' by.

After a pause, KAREEM starts to whistle a tune: 'Eye of the Tiger'. He does so for quite some time, dancing in his seat, building to a great climax – when at last IMAN turns around again.

IMAN: *(A feat of superhuman courage.)* I'd like you to give me my pen back please.

KAREEM: *(Yawns.)* …Tired now.

Short pause.

KAREEM: You say somethin'?

IMAN: Give me my pen back.

Short pause.

KAREEM: I'm sorry, what?

IMAN: You took my pen. Give it – Can I have it back please?

KAREEM: Oh…This *your* pen?

IMAN: Yes.

KAREEM: Oh. God. I'm sorry. I am so sorry, Iman. I didn't realise. Silly me.

Short pause.

IMAN: Can I have it back please?

KAREEM: Huh? Oh…No…No, you can't. You cannot have your pen back.

Short pause.

KAREEM: It's okay though. Your mum said I could have it. Last night. She said it. After I…you know, after I fucked her. Yeah, last night, after I fucked your mum, she said, 'Kareem, you know what? That was *so good*, just *so good*, as a small token of my gratitude, I'd like you to have my little Iman's pen. You take it off of him at school tomorrow, and if he gives you any trouble, you tell him that I prefer you anyway, because you give me such deep, intense pleasure, and really he's just a whiny, pathetic little bitch…' That's what she said. Which – Bit harsh, I felt. Also, I didn't actually think it *was* that good. *I* was, obviously – manz was formidable. I mean, she screamed like – The woman is bare loud, innit – Hope we didn't wake you, by the way – But, no, her actual – her performance itself – not so much. Kinda like a loose, wet glove –

IMAN: *(Quietly.)* Stop it –

KAREEM: No, swear down, man. Not sure if I'll – again, to be honest. Time to move on, I think. Upgrade. Yeah… If I *did* though – go back, I mean – for more sweet mom action, if it became like a, like a thing, I'd be your stepdad, wouldn't I? – *(Continues.)*

IMAN: *(Overlaps, quietly.)* Shut up –

KAREEM: – Which, now that I think of it, I'm not sure I'm ready for that. I mean, not yet.

Beat.

KAREEM: Did you just tell me to shut up?

MISS whirlwinds through the door – then stops abruptly. Papers, folders, a teacher's planner, and a laptop with its power cord dangling precariously spill from her arms. Beat.

MISS: *(Perplexed.)* There's only two of you.

KAREEM: *(All sunshine.)* Hi, miss.

MISS: Hi, Kareem. Where are the others?

KAREEM: Others, miss? What others? *(Silly Spanish voice.)* Los otros no aqui.

MISS sighs, dumps all she's carrying on one of the desks.

MISS: There's supposed to be four of you…?

KAREEM: Is there? Wait. *(Points finger at himself.)* One. *(Points finger at IMAN.)* Two. *(Turns, points his finger, ready to count a third person, then 'realises' there's no one else there.)* Oh… *(Turns back to MISS, shakes his head gravely.)* No, miss –

MISS: *(Sighs.)* Let me – just…

She picks up her planner, flicks through it in search of a piece of paper with the names of the four students she was expecting to see here in front of her. It takes her some time – her planner is crammed with pieces of paper and she's trying her best not to seem harassed – but eventually she finds what she's looking for.

MISS: Ah, there we are…Now I just need…

She looks for a pen –

KAREEM: *(Stands up, goes to her.)* Pen, miss?

MISS: *(Takes the pen – IMAN's pen.)* Thank you. At least one of us is prepared. So. *(Ticks off his name.)* Kareem, you're here. Obviously.

KAREEM: *(Extravagant.)* Yes!

MISS: Unmistakably. *(To IMAN.)* And you are…?

IMAN: Iman.

MISS: Iman. *(Ticks off his name.)* Okay. So, no Muhammed?

IMAN: …

KAREEM: …

MISS: Anybody know anything about Muhammed?

Short pause.

KAREEM: He's Muslim, miss.

MISS: What?

KAREEM: I'm pretty sure, with a name like that – with a name like Muhammed – I think we can *infer* that he's Muslim.

MISS: Kareem, I don't care if he's Muslim. I don't care if he's the actual, historical prophet Muhammed. He failed GCSE English. He needs to be in this room. Where is he?

KAREEM: No idea, miss. Haven't seen him.

MISS: Okay. Thank you, Kareem.

KAREEM: You're welcome –

MISS: And Alisha? Any clues?

IMAN: …

KAREEM: *(Shrugs.)* …?

MISS: No. Excellent. So – two of you are missing. Wonderful start. Fantastic. Here's your pen, Kareem.

KAREEM: Thanks, miss –

MISS: Right. Okay. We'll lurch feebly on, then, shall we, the three of us –

A knock on the door.

MISS: *(Calls out.)* Come in.

The door opens cautiously. ALISHA peeks in – she's beautiful. KAREEM clocks her immediately.

ALISHA: Excuse me, miss, is this –

MISS: Yes, it certainly is. Are you Alisha?

ALISHA: *(Comes in.)* Yes, miss.

MISS: Why are you late?

ALISHA: …I don't know, miss.

MISS: …You don't know…? You do not know why you are late?

ALISHA: …

MISS: May God have mercy on us all – you are a sentient being, are you not? Surely you must have some inkling of your own whereabouts in the moments prior to your entering this room…What happened…?

ALISHA: …I couldn't find the room.

MISS: You couldn't find the room?

ALISHA: No, miss.

MISS: I see…Well, that alarms me, Alisha. That perturbs me. Do you know what that word means – perturbs?

ALISHA: No, miss.

MISS: No…It means, 'Eighty per cent of success is showing up', Alisha. That's what it means. Someone successful said that. I can't remember who. The / point is –

IMAN: *(Quietly.)* Woody Allen.

MISS: What's that?

IMAN: It was Woody Allen who said it, miss.

MISS: Woody Allen? There you go. He's won an Oscar.

IMAN: *Four* Oscars.

MISS: Four Oscars?

IMAN: Yes, miss –

KAREEM: I swear he's a paedophile –

MISS: That's not the point –

IMAN: *(Without facing KAREEM.)* He is *not* a paedophile –

KAREEM: I swear he married his own daughter –

MISS: It's not the point –

IMAN: She wasn't his daughter –

KAREEM: Probably what he meant was eighty per cent of success is showin' up *at the playground* –

MISS: Kareem, stop talking –

IMAN: He doesn't go to the playground –

KAREEM: And anyway, miss, Alisha *did* show up. Just a few minutes late. So, technically, she still has like a, like a seventy-eight per cent chance of success, seventy-nine even –

MISS: THAT IS NOT THE POINT!

Short pause.

MISS: I want you to listen to me now, okay, all of you.

Short pause.

MISS: For the next six weeks, we meet here. In this room. At this time. You need to be here. On time. Without fail. Unless you are hospitalised, or deceased, or suffering some kind of catastrophic physical or emotional trauma, you need to *be here.* You need to be ready to work the moment I walk in that door. *Before* I walk in the door. Do you understand me?

KAREEM/IMAN/ALISHA: *(Together.)* Yes, miss.

MISS: Alisha?

ALISHA: Yes, miss.

MISS: Good. *(To all of them.)* Look, maybe you don't understand how precarious your position is here? Okay, so let me spell it out to you…

None of you should be at this school right now. Simple as that. You should not be here. The only reason you are here – some…person – I don't know who – whoever it was enrolled you, frankly…they screwed up. They should not have let you in. Students who fail GCSE English do not gain admission to our sixth form. They do not.

And yet here you are.

And here I am.

You are extremely lucky, all of you. You're lucky Mr Banks is a kind man. He could have kicked you out. He could. As soon as the enrolment error came to light. Instead, he's given you an opportunity. He's done you a kindness. But do not be mistaken. This is not a hand-out. You have not been redeemed.

You have six weeks – *six short weeks* – to do what is, in effect, a two-year course. A course that you have already managed to fail. And this time you have to do it alongside the even greater challenge of your AS subjects. That is a mountain, people. You need to start climbing.

You will see me once a week. Possibly twice. If they agree to cover my PSHE lessons. Either way the onus here is *on you*. Unless *you* put in the effort this time, *you* will fail. And if you do, it is adios Kansas. You will no longer be a student at this sixth form. This is your one and only shot. Capish…?

KAREEM/IMAN/ALISHA: …

MISS: Do you get what I'm saying to you?

KAREEM/IMAN/ALISHA: *(Together.)* Yes, miss.

MISS: Excellent. Sit down, Alisha.

ALISHA goes to sit down.

MISS: Sorry, hang on…That skirt…

ALISHA stops, looks at MISS.

MISS: *(Shakes her head.)* No.

ALISHA: Excuse me, miss?

MISS: Too short.

ALISHA: …?

MISS: It contravenes the school dress code…I see you wearing it again, I send you home.

ALISHA: …Okay…Sorry, miss.

MISS gestures for ALISHA to sit down. ALISHA does so.

MISS: Right. Before we go any further, get your diaries out please. I want you to make a note: by next week, you need to be ready to do your individual speaking and listening assessment. This time next week, we're recording those speeches. The topic is completely up to you. I'll give you a sheet in a moment with all the details, but I want you to note it down now – individual speeches, next Wednesday. *Be ready.*

Also, for next week, I'd like to see a draft of your narrative coursework. You'll remember there are three pieces to do, but I want you to focus on the narrative first of all. So, for Wednesday *as well*, a full first draft of that to be handed in please. *Do not*, however, under any circumstances, give me a story about a hitman, or a bank robber, or a car chase, or a kidnapping, or a mild-mannered chemistry teacher who becomes a ruthless drug baron. If you want a good grade for this, mine your own personal experience. Write something honest. That is the key.

Okay.

Any questions so far?

Immediately, KAREEM raises his hand.

MISS: Yes, Kareem.

KAREEM: Miss, if he *is* the actual prophet Muhammed, will he still have to do the retake?

Short pause. MISS gives KAREEM the death stare – but he chooses not to take the hint.

KAREEM: Also – these are less questions, more…points of information – but, first off, it's kind of our second shot – *(Continues.)*

MISS: *(Overlaps.)* Stop talking, Kareem –

KAREEM: – You said it's our one and only shot, but we've already had a shot and we failed, so, technically – second shot. *Moreover*, it's not called AS anymore – *(Continues.)*

MISS: *(Overlaps.)* Stop talking –

KAREEM: Or PSHE, for that matter. It's PSH*CE…E*. They added *two* new letters. A 'C' and an 'E'. PSH*CEE*. With a quack quack here and a moo moo there. And, finally, it was Mr Campbell who enrolled me. You might want to have a quiet word.

Beat.

MISS: Step outside a minute please, Kareem.

KAREEM: …

MISS: *Now.*

KAREEM: Sure thing, miss.

KAREEM gets up and goes out.

MISS: *(To the others.)* …I'll be back in one moment.

MISS goes out. A long pause. IMAN and ALISHA sit in a silent chasm of awkwardness. ALISHA is a little rattled after the drubbing she received from MISS. IMAN is just IMAN: massively uncomfortable. On one or two occasions, it appears that he might be about to say something, but he just can't get the words out. Eventually, after a great internal struggle, he finds the resolve to speak…

IMAN: Do you like Woody Allen?

Short pause.

ALISHA: Sorry, what?

IMAN: …Woody Allen? Do you like him – / his –

ALISHA: Woody Allen?

IMAN: …Uh, yeah…

ALISHA: I don't know who that is.

IMAN: …Oh.

An awkward silence.

IMAN: He's a film-maker.

ALISHA smiles politely – she's not interested in Woody Allen. Another awkward silence.

IMAN: He's not a, uh…He's not what Kareem said he was.

ALISHA: Right.

Short pause.

ALISHA: What did Kareem say he was?

IMAN: He said he was a, uh…Like a…Never mind.

Short pause.

ALISHA: *('What is with this guy?')* Okay.

Another silence.

ALISHA: Kareem is the *(Gestures toward the door.)*…?

IMAN: What? Oh, uh…yeah, that guy.

Another silence. IMAN is in agony – should he tell her his name now…? He deliberates – it takes some time, but he finally works up the courage –

IMAN: My name / is –

The door opens again. KAREEM enters, followed by MISS. KAREEM goes back to his seat.

MISS: *(As she enters.)* Right. You two. Folders.

MISS gives a folder each to KAREEM and IMAN.

MISS: Alisha, I haven't got yours, obviously. Why don't you hop on one of the computers and get started? I need to go grab another laptop from somewhere –

ALISHA: Miss, would it be alright if I went to the toilet quickly?

Short pause. MISS gives ALISHA the death stare.

ALISHA: Sorry, miss, I really need to go. I'll be super-fast.

Short pause.

MISS: You have two minutes.

ALISHA: Thank you.

ALISHA hurries out.

MISS: Gentlemen, start reading your last attempt at the narrative. Work out what you need to do to improve, yes?

MISS goes out. IMAN opens his folder. KAREEM pauses a moment, then stands up, goes to the door, looks through the glass panel, then turns –

KAREEM: *(American accent.)* Damn. Da-ham. She is, like, mmm-mmmm. Damn girl. You sumptin'. You fahn. You miiighty fahn. *(Normal voice.)* Did you see her, freshie? Did you? *(American accent.)* She is smokin'. *(Normal voice.)* Don't tell your mum, obviously. Wouldn't want to hurt her feelin's. *(American accent.)* But damn. Damn Alisha. You fahn. You sweet like cahndy. I mean –

He whistles.

KAREEM: *(Sings in Marvin Gaye falsetto.)* 'And if you feel, like I feel, sugah, oh, huh, oh, come on, owww, let's get it on.' *(American accent.)* We talkin' off the scale. I wanna peel her like a banana. How's a man supposed to concentrate when they be danglin' this honey pot all up in yo' grill? I for one am glad I failed me some English. Gonna be failin' all up again in this mothafucka, this the reward I get. Mercy. Mercy me. Coffee and pie. My oh my. Damn.

Short pause.

KAREEM: Damn.

Beat – KAREEM calms down, goes back to his desk, picks up his folder, skims through it half-heartedly. Beat.

KAREEM: Oi, what you writin' your story about, freshie?

IMAN ignores him.

KAREEM: Iman…? Oh, Iman…? What you writin' your story about?

IMAN continues to ignore him.

KAREEM: *(Posh BBC nature programme voice.)* It seems to have lost its tongue.

ALISHA returns.

KAREEM: *(Barry White voice.)* Hi.

ALISHA: *(Sits down, aloof.)* Hi.

Short pause.

KAREEM: *(American accent.)* My name's George. This here's Lennie. He ain't much of a talker, but he buck barley with the strength of fo' men. You ain't never seen nothin' like it.

ALISHA: *(Unimpressed.)* …

KAREEM: *(Normal voice.)* Jokes…Just jokes.

ALISHA: …

KAREEM: Kareem's the name. But most people call me *(Barry White voice)* The Love Doctor.

ALISHA: *(A cold smile.)* …

KAREEM: Alisha, right?

ALISHA: Yes.

KAREEM: *(Holds out his hand.)* The pleasure is all mine.

Short pause. ALISHA doesn't respond.

KAREEM: *(Retracts his hand.)* Safe.

An awkward pause.

KAREEM: So you're new then, yeah?

ALISHA: Yes. You're very observant.

KAREEM: Oh, I am. I am. And I like what I be observin' right now, you feel me?

ALISHA: …

KAREEM: Anyway…

Another awkward pause.

KAREEM: That's a, eh, I noticed your necklace there. Very nice.

Short pause.

KAREEM: What is that – the, eh –

ALISHA: It's called a 'mind your own fuckin' business'.

KAREEM: Ah. I see. Not familiar with that particular, eh –

MISS returns with a laptop which she gives to IMAN.

MISS: *(As she enters.)* Okay, here we go…

KAREEM: Oh, hey miss. Long time no see.

MISS: Right, let's get a move on, you lot. Kareem, you can take the DeLorean.

MISS gives KAREEM an old, chunky laptop from the teacher's desk. IMAN laughs to himself in acknowledgement of MISS's 'Back to the Future' reference. KAREEM gives IMAN a look of derision before –

KAREEM: Thanks, miss.

Short pause. KAREEM scribbles something on the piece of paper he took out earlier.

KAREEM: Miss, could I borrow a pen please? *(American accent.)* This pen here. This a terrible pen. I's ashamed to call this mah pen.

MISS gives him the death stare.

KAREEM: Sorry, miss.

Short pause.

KAREEM: Seriously, though, anybody got a pen I could borrow?

Blackout.

SCENE TWO

The next day.

MISS sits at the teacher's desk with a set of exercise books, one of which is open in front of her. She hovers over it with a red pen, making the occasional tick, circling errors, writing comments.

All is silent – until suddenly –

MISS: *(Addresses the exercise book.)* Fuck me, child. Priestley. *Priestley.* L-*E*-Y. It's on the cover of the fucking book right in front of you. How difficult can it be?

> *She goes back to marking silently, until she emits a disgruntled sigh, circles something vigorously, writes a comment.*

MISS: *(Matter-of-fact, as she writes in the book.)* Dear parent, your child is an illiterate fuckwit. Please refrain from further procreation at all costs. Yours faithfully, the Education System *(trails off in the middle of 'system')* –

> *She drops her pen. Beat. She looks up at the ceiling. She looks down at the floor – then back at the ceiling. She stands up, moves away from the desk, thinks for a moment – then gets up on a chair or one of the student desks to take a closer look at the ceiling.*

> *A knock on the door.*

MISS: *(Calls out.)* Yes…? *(Impatient.)* Come in.

> *IMAN shuffles in nervously.*

IMAN: Excuse me, miss –

MISS: *(Still looking at the ceiling, holds out a hand.)* One second.

> *Short pause. MISS continues to inspect the ceiling. IMAN stands awkwardly by the door.*

MISS: Can you hear that?

> *Short pause.*

IMAN: …Uh, no…?

MISS: Listen carefully.

Short pause.

MISS: Come closer. Don't make any noise. Just listen.

Short pause.

MISS: Can you hear it?

IMAN: …?

MISS: That is the sound…of apathy.

Short pause. She looks at IMAN. He seems unsure as to whether there is an actual sound he should be able to identify.

MISS: *(Comes down off the chair/desk, points at the stain on the ceiling tiles.)* Leak number one, look. See the stain. Water comes through the ceiling whenever it rains. I reported that in May. To a wall of indifference. *May.* That's four months ago. *Five.* And now today I unveil to you – the all new leak number two. *(Moves the bin so that it catches the water from the new leak.)* It's not even raining, but, by Jove, they've gone and done it again. This place is crumbling, Imran, and nobody gives a – *(instead of 'fuck')* fudge.

Beat.

MISS: *(Faux cheerful.)* How can I help you on this joyous afternoon?

IMAN: …Um…Sorry to disturb you, miss. Just, I had an idea for my narrative and I wanted to check it. With you. Before I started to, uhm –

MISS: Oh yes. Good. What is it? Shoot.

IMAN: …Uh. Well. Basically, it's about a young boy and his first trip to the cinema. With, uh, with his father…

MISS: …Right. That sounds… *(A euphemism for 'dull'.)* Interesting…

IMAN: …

MISS: Does anything happen in the story or – I mean, he goes to the cinema…?

17

IMAN: Yeah…Well, no. Not exactly. He's actually – he's at the cinema already. In the – now. In the present. He's, like, sitting in his seat. With, I don't know, his mum, or, whoever. Before the movie starts. But he's thinking about another time. He's remembering. His first trip to the cinema. With his dad. And, uh, he's kind of…he's upset, but he doesn't say anything. He just sort of keeps it to himself, and his mum never finds out what's really going on beneath the surface.

MISS: …Okay…So that's…What is going on beneath the surface exactly?

IMAN: …?

MISS: Why is he upset?

IMAN: Oh. Yeah, um. He, uh…He misses his father.

MISS: Right. So his father's not…?

IMAN: No.

MISS: No. Okay. So he – the boy – he wants to…? Remember we said that – make your character want something.

IMAN: Yeah. He wants to, uh, like, relive the…Go back. He wants to be there again. With his dad. But he can't, because it's just a memory. It's gone, so…

MISS: I see.

IMAN: …Yeah…

Short pause.

IMAN: Do you think that's – Does it sound okay?

Another knock on the door.

MISS: Sorry, let me – *(Calls out.)* Come in please.

ALISHA enters.

ALISHA: Hi, miss –

MISS: Hi, Alisha.

ALISHA: Excuse me. Am I interruptin' – ?

MISS: No, it's fine. What can I do for you? Nice trousers, by the way.

ALISHA: What? Oh. Thank you. Em, this is gonna sound really bad, miss, but, eh, you know that sheet with the details of the speakin' and listenin'…thing? The one you gave us yesterday…?

MISS: Yes.

ALISHA: I was wonderin' if I could possibly get another copy. Please. I kinda lost mine.

MISS: It doesn't *sound* bad.

ALISHA: What –

MISS: It *is* bad.

ALISHA: …Sorry, miss.

MISS: …If the exam was on first impressions, Alisha…

ALISHA: …

MISS: *(Looks.)* I haven't got a spare sheet here, I don't think… Could you – Do you know where the English office is?

ALISHA: …

MISS: No, of course, you don't. *(Sighs.)* Fine. I'll run out. Fetch another one for you. Like a dog.

ALISHA: Thanks, miss. Sorry.

MISS makes a sour face then goes out. ALISHA barks, flicks two fingers in the direction of the door then turns –

ALISHA: Hey Iman.

IMAN: Oh. Hey.

ALISHA: How are you?

IMAN: Okay. Thanks.

Short, uncomfortable pause. IMAN waits too long before asking –

IMAN: How are you?

ALISHA: Yeah. Good. You know.

IMAN: …Yeah.

IMAN nods. After another awkward pause –

IMAN: You know my name.

ALISHA: *(Weirded out.)* …Eh, yeah…

IMAN: …No, because, uh, miss just called me 'Imran'. Like, with an 'R'.

ALISHA: Oh. I get you. That sucks.

IMAN nods again.

ALISHA: Man, I hate it when teachers do that. It's like, learn my name, bitch. I'm not some interchangeable exam monkey. I'm an actual person.

IMAN: *(Over-enthusiastic.)* I know…

He doesn't quite know what to say next – another weird pause.

ALISHA: Did you correct her?

IMAN: …Uh…like…?

ALISHA: Did you tell her your real name?

IMAN: …Oh, not – no.

ALISHA: You should tell her your real name. You need to stand up for yourself, Iman.

IMAN: …Okay…

Short pause.

IMAN: Did you stand up for yourself?

ALISHA: …What?

IMAN: Just now. When she told you off about the – about losing the sheet –

ALISHA: …That was different.

IMAN: Ah. I see…Was it?

ALISHA: Yes. It was totally *(unsaid: 'different')…*

> *IMAN nods some more. After a short pause –*

IMAN: What about yesterday? With the skirt –

ALISHA: *(Half-smiling.)* Look, shut the fuck up, okay. Nobody asked you.

IMAN: Sorry. Sorry. You're right. Nobody…yep…

> *Short pause. IMAN tries to contain a smile.*

IMAN: Those *are* nice trousers, by the way –

ALISHA: Alright, okay. God. Point taken…She is kind of a bitch though, right? Or is it just me she hates?

IMAN: Um, actually, it *is* just you.

ALISHA: …You're like – funny, Iman!

IMAN: …I am?

ALISHA: Yes. You act all quiet and shit, but actually you're real funny.

IMAN: Oh –

ALISHA: I like it.

> *MISS returns with the information sheet. During the following short exchange, IMAN struggles not to burst with unspoken joy –*

MISS: *(As she enters.)* Right, Alisha, one replacement sheet for you.

ALISHA: *(Takes the sheet.)* Oh, thank you, miss.

MISS: Don't lose this one.

ALISHA: I won't. I promise.

> *Short pause.*

MISS: You look weirdly happy, Imran?

IMAN: …Uh, no…This is just my normal facc.

MISS: Ah. Excellent…Well, if there's nothing else…

ALISHA: Yeah, I gotta cut –

MISS: Yep. See you on Wednesday, Alisha. On time.

ALISHA: On time, miss. See you then. *(Deliberately emphasising the correct pronunciation of his name.)* Later, Iman.

IMAN: Bye, Alisha.

ALISHA goes to leave – then stops.

ALISHA: Oh, actually, Iman, would you be my partner for the paired speakin' and listenin'?

Short pause.

IMAN: …Huh…?

ALISHA: Wanna do the paired task together – you and me?

Short pause.

IMAN: Yes!

ALISHA: Okay –

IMAN: Awesome! Thank you. I mean, yeah, that would be – yeah.

ALISHA: Great. Well, wanna come common room with me now? We can work out a practice schedule.

IMAN: *(Can't quite believe this is happening.)* …We…Yes. Okay. A practice schedule.

ALISHA: Safe –

IMAN: Uhm, about my story, miss –

MISS: It sounds good, Imran. I look forward to reading it.

IMAN: …Oh. Okay. Thank you…Uh, miss, my name is Iman.

MISS: …Excuse me?

IMAN: …There's no 'R'. It's just 'Iman'. Not 'Imran'.

MISS: …Iman?

IMAN: Yes.

MISS: …Ah. Apologies.

IMAN: That's okay…Bye, miss.

MISS forces a smile. IMAN and ALISHA leave. MISS's smile turns into a wince of embarrassment at her error. Beat. A drop of water falls. MISS looks up at the ceiling.

MISS: *(Addresses the ceiling.)* Fuck you.

Blackout.

SCENE THREE

The following week.

KAREEM is standing at the head of the classroom. He starts to speak immediately at lights up. A small audio recorder rests on a desk in front of him. MISS is sitting at one of the student desks, pen in hand, a notepad and a piece of paper in front of her. She jots things down in the notepad as KAREEM speaks. IMAN and ALISHA are each sitting at one of the desks.

KAREEM: *(With great theatricality.)* Ladies and gentlemens.

Allow me to introduce myself. My name is Kareem Al Habsi Haribo Smith (also known as The Love Doctor) and I am your MC for the evenin'. At tonight's meetin' we's gonna be discussin' an issue of devastatin' importance, a nightmarish threat to our community, our families, and, worst of all, our children. And our children's children. And our children's children's children. This threat is inflicted on us by none other than the devil hisself. *Satan. (Sings.)* Dun dun duuuuh.

Yes, my friends, you guessed it, tonight we's talkin' about…celebrity paedophiles.

MISS looks up from her notes.

KAREEM: Now, I know what you're thinking, folks: hold on a minute, Kareem – the British people is very fond of their rich and famous bredren. Okay. Okay. But have you thought about this, Britain? *(With sudden force.)* Perverts like Jimmy Saville, Willy Allen – *(Continues.)*

MISS: *(Overlaps.)* Stop.

KAREEM: – and that creepy Australian cartoon guy – *(Continues.)*

MISS: *(Overlaps.)* Kareem, stop –

KAREEM: – are hypnotisin' our children with their magic flutes – *(Continues.)*

MISS: *(Overlaps.)* End of recording. Stop.

MISS presses 'Stop' on the audio recorder.

KAREEM: There a problem, miss?

MISS: *(Calm.)* Sit down, Kareem.

KAREEM: Kinda in the middle of my speech here –

MISS: No, you're not. Sit down.

KAREEM: Uh, okay, miss, I don't mean to / like –

MISS: *(Still calm but growing increasingly firm.)* Yes, Kareem, there is a problem. Celebrity paedophiles. That's a problem. It's a wildly inappropriate topic for a GCSE speech.

KAREEM: Oh.

MISS: Yes.

KAREEM: You want me to tone it down a smidge?

MISS: No, Kareem, I don't want you to tone it down a smidge. I want you to tear it up and throw it in the bin, okay. I want you to start over. With a new topic – *(Continues.)*

KAREEM: *(Overlaps.)* Miss, man –

MISS: – And I want you to stop treating this like a joke.

KAREEM: I weren't treating nothing like a joke –

MISS: No? Really?

KAREEM: No –

MISS: Look, just sit down, alright. You and I are going to have some serious words at the end of this session –

KAREEM rolls his eyes or tuts or makes some other gesture of mild defiance.

MISS: Imran, you're up next.

ALISHA: His name's Iman, miss.

MISS: Iman. Sorry. Iman…Kareem, I said sit down.

KAREEM: *(Sits down.)* Alright, okay.

Short pause.

MISS: *(Urging him to go to the front of the class.)* Iman.

IMAN stands up, goes to the front, removes a piece of paper.

MISS: Nice, lively delivery, please. If you make a mistake, don't worry about it. Just keep going.

IMAN nods.

MISS: All set?

IMAN: Uh, I guess.

MISS presses 'Record' on the audio device and reels off this –

MISS: Green Hill High School. Centre number 13767. Cambridge IGCSE. First Language English, 0522, Component 6, speaking and listening. Examiner: Miss Murphy. Date: September 28th 2016. Candidate name…

MISS points to IMAN.

IMAN: Iman Bahamanabadi.

MISS: Candidate number…

IMAN: Two-one-six-seven.

MISS steps back and gestures for IMAN to start his speech.

IMAN: *(Nervously.)* Good afternoon.

Short pause. IMAN clears his throat.

IMAN: *(Reads in stilted monotone from the piece of paper.)* My speech is about the film, *Back to the Future.*

Short pause.

IMAN: *Back to the Future* was released in 1985.

Short pause.

IMAN: It was directed by Robert Zem – Zemeckis and starred Michael J. Fox and Christopher / Lloyd –

MISS: Stop. Stop. *(Goes to the audio recorder, presses 'Stop'.)* End of recording.

Short pause.

MISS: Iman, could you liven up your delivery, please? Before the rest of us expire.

IMAN: *(Embarrassed.)* …

MISS: Who are you speaking to?

IMAN: …

MISS: Who are your audience?

IMAN: …Uh, I'm not really sure, miss.

MISS: No. Well, if you speak to them like that, they're all going to pack up and leave. What's the purpose of the speech?

IMAN: …Um, to talk about…I'm not sure.

MISS: Did I not say this to you last week?

IMAN: …

MISS: Purpose? Audience?

IMAN: …Yes.

MISS: So…? What happened?

IMAN: …Could I work on it a little more, miss? I can come after school tomorrow to record it.

MISS: Oh you can, can you? You can bleed away another few minutes of my life, hah?

IMAN: …I don't feel ready today, miss. The speech isn't good enough.

MISS: No, it's not.

Short pause.

MISS: Fine. Tomorrow it is then. I expect it to be a lot better by then, Iman, okay?

IMAN nods, sits down.

MISS: Right, Alisha. You're up.

ALISHA smiles awkwardly, stands up, goes to the front.

MISS: No notes?

ALISHA shakes her head.

MISS: You know what you're doing?

ALISHA: Yes, miss.

MISS: Okay. Ready?

ALISHA breathes, then nods 'Yes' again, MISS presses 'Record' on the audio device and recites this, bored –

MISS: Green Hill High School. Centre number 13767. Cambridge IGCSE. First Language English, 0522, Component 6, speaking and listening. Examiner: Miss Murphy. Date: September 28th 2016. Candidate name –

MISS points to ALISHA.

ALISHA: Alisha Soneji.

MISS: Candidate number…

ALISHA: Two-zero-five-seven.

MISS steps back and gestures for ALISHA to start her speech. MISS makes notes as ALISHA speaks, but, as the speech goes on, MISS loses interest in the notes and just listens.

ALISHA: Parents. Governors. Head Teacher…

When you look at the person standin' before you now, who do you see? *What* do you see? Do I look like a number to you? Do I look like a grade? A statistic? A set of data? Five A star to C grades? Do I look like a failure…? I am none of these things.

I am a human bein'. I have a heartbeat. An imagination. A conscience. I am not a failure. I am not a number. I am not a grade…Am I?

This is a number…Sixteen. That's how old I was the first time I was obliged to take this exam. *Sixteen* years old. I was a child. I *am* a child. And you branded me a failure. I failed, you said. 'You are a failure.' Well, maybe that's wrong. Maybe *you* are the failures. How about that? Maybe *you* failed *me.*

'Think for yourself,' you said. 'And while you're at it, tuck your shirt in, and do your top button up…' You fools. Don't you see the contradiction? This is not a school. You're not teachin' me nothin'. I'm not learnin'.

A robot factory. That's all you got here. A boot camp for exam soldiers. But I'm not fightin' your war. I'm not wearin' your ugly, uncomfortable uniform no more. I'm not gonna allow you to stifle me. I'm not gonna allow you to oppress me. I am a seventeen-year-old girl. I got things to say. I got places to go. I got dreams I ain't even aware of yet. I am not gonna be one of your obedient little soldiers.

Short pause.

ALISHA: Except, of course, I am. Ain't I? I'm playin' the game right now. I'm standin' in a classroom. I'm wearin' the clothes you told me to wear. I addressed you earlier on: my audience. 'Parents. Governors. Head Teacher,' I said. But there are no parents, no governors, no head teacher. These people are not my audience. I am not speakin' to them. I am speakin' to a voice recorder. I am speakin' to 'the examiner'. A man or woman I've never met – will never meet – but who gets paid to colour my dreams. To determine the places I can go.

'Think for yourself,' they said. Nah. This is it for me now. Two-zero-five-seven, reportin' for duty. This time I'm gonna succeed. Whatever that means. End of recordin'.

ALISHA presses 'Stop' on the audio recorder and walks back to her seat. An awed silence before IMAN starts clapping.

MISS: Alright –

IMAN: That was awesome.

KAREEM: That *was* awesome.

KAREEM and IMAN look to MISS for her verdict.

MISS: Right, well, interesting, I'll give you that. Some grammatical errors, but, yeah, overall, not too bad.

IMAN: It was better than 'not too bad'.

KAREEM: Was bangin'.

ALISHA: What mark would it get, miss?

Beat.

MISS: Why are you here, Alisha? If that's what you're capable of. Why didn't you just do that last year?

All eyes are on ALISHA. She's embarrassed.

Blackout.

SCENE FOUR

About forty-five minutes later.

MISS is standing. KAREEM is slumped in a chair, avoiding eye contact with her.

Silence, until –

MISS: Sit up properly, will you, please?

> *KAREEM adjusts his body position slightly. Short pause.*

MISS: *Properly*, please.

> *KAREEM sits bolt upright, exaggeratedly rigid and stiff. Short pause.*

MISS: Look at me.

> *KAREEM refuses to look at her. Short pause.*

MISS: Kareem, you're seventeen years old…Look at me.

> *KAREEM looks at her. MISS holds eye contact in silence for a moment before –*

MISS: How long have we known each other?

> *KAREEM shrugs.*

MISS: I'm trying to remember – you were in Year 8, right? When I taught you? What's that, five years ago…? I'm wondering if you've grown up at all in that time…?

KAREEM: …

> *Beat.*

MISS: What do you want to do with your life, Kareem?

KAREEM: Not this again.

MISS: Yes, this again. What do you want to do with your life?

KAREEM: McDonald's, miss.

> *Short pause.*

MISS: McDonald's?

KAREEM: Yep. I wanna flip me some burgers.

Short pause.

MISS: You don't want to go to university?

KAREEM: Nah, man, my brother went uni. Now he's unemployed. And in debt. He does online poker all day, in his boxer shorts. That ain't for me. McDonald's is my spiritual home.

MISS: Okay, well, did you know that for any job, even for a job at your spiritual home, you need to have GCSE English?

KAREEM: What do you mean *even*? Why you hatin' on Mickey D's? They fine dinin'. Happy Meals. Ronald McDonald –

MISS: *(Ignoring him.)* Did you know that for any job, even at McDonald's, you will need to have GCSE English?

KAREEM: Did you ever work at McDonald's?

MISS: *(Sighs.)* You're not taking this seriously, are you?

KAREEM: I am takin' it seriously. I'm *(mispronounces the word)* aksin' you a serious question: did you ever work at McDonald's? Because if you did, yeah, you might be able to advise me on my chosen career path –

MISS: Okay. Perhaps we should go to Mr Banks' office? Maybe you'd take him seriously. *Or*, in fact, how about we arrange for your parents to come in and we, all of us – you, me, Mr Banks, Mr and Mrs Tamam – we all sit down and talk about how to move you on out of here and into burger university? How would you like that?

Short pause.

KAREEM: I wouldn't like that, miss. That don't sound too swell.

MISS: *(Goes to leave.)* No, well, that's exactly what's going to happen, Kareem, because I have had enough –

KAREEM: Hold up, miss. Hold up. Hold up.

MISS stops. Beat.

KAREEM: Don't go to Mr Banks, miss…Don't call my parents. Please.

MISS: Why not?

Short pause.

KAREEM: Because. They'll get upset.

Short pause.

KAREEM: Give me one more chance. Please, miss.

MISS: There are no more one-more-chances for you, Kareem. You're all out of luck –

KAREEM: Miss, I beg you, don't call my dad. He'll go batshit. *(Meaning sorry for swearing.)* Sorry…Seriously, miss. Don't call him. He's, like, not in a good place right now.

Beat.

MISS: I want you here Friday after school, ready to perform your speech.

KAREEM: Okay –

MISS: Not some immature joke. A nice, appropriate, inoffensive speech. Understood?

KAREEM: Yes, miss.

MISS: By next Wednesday, I want to see a full draft of your narrative *and* a full draft of one of the other two pieces –

KAREEM: Got it, miss. I'm writin' it down. Could I borrow a pen please?

Short pause. Then, with a withering look, MISS gives him a pen. KAREEM responds with a nod of thanks then writes in his diary.

MISS: If you screw up, if you let me down, I am on the phone straight away. I'm not even going to discuss it with you. I am on speed dial to Mr Tamam. Clear?

KAREEM: Clear, miss. I won't let you down. I won't let myself down. I don't wanna end up at like Burger King or KFC. It's McDonald's for me. All the way.

Short pause – MISS is not impressed.

KAREEM: Jokes, miss.

MISS: Do you understand how serious I am?

KAREEM: I really do, miss.

MISS: Good. You should leave now, Kareem, before you say something to change my mind.

KAREEM: I'm gone, miss. Can I *(mispronounces the word)* aks you something first though?

Short pause.

MISS: What is it?

KAREEM: Do you like your job?

MISS: What?

KAREEM: Nah, cos I know you took a break last year, for a while, what's it called, a sabbatical, yeah, so I was just wondering, do you like it?

Short pause.

MISS: It's not really appropriate for you to ask me that question, Kareem.

KAREEM: …Oh –

MISS: What do you care anyway?

KAREEM: I care, miss. I care. I worry.

MISS: Oh you worry, do you? You worry about me?

KAREEM: Yeah. I worry about your emotional and psychological well-being –

MISS: *(Laughs.)* Ha! I'm sure you do.

KAREEM: I do, man. Cos like you seem kinda…pissed off. Sometimes. Not like all the time. But sometimes. Like you need a visit to the Moroccan spa. You know, massage. Facial. Ben and Jerry's.

MISS: …I am pissed off sometimes, Kareem. With students like you.

KAREEM: No. I can see that. I would be pissed off with me too, yeah, if I was you. I would spend like every day at the Moroccan spa…You ain't answered my question though, miss…Do you like your job?

MISS: Like I said, not appropriate.

KAREEM: *(Nods.)* Interesting. That means you don't like it.

MISS: No, it doesn't. It means it's not…professional for me to talk to students about such matters –

KAREEM: Nah, but if you liked it, you'd be all open, innit. Like, *(a bad imitation of her voice)* 'Oh, yes, young man, I feel so fulfilled. I make the little buds grow.'

MISS: You should go now, Kareem.

KAREEM: I think you should quit.

MISS: …Pardon me?

KAREEM: No offence, miss, but like your job is bullshit. You should quit.

MISS: …

KAREEM: I don't mean teachin' is bullshit. I mean what teachin' has *become* is / bullshit –

MISS: Okay, Kareem, I'm taking offence. For one thing, stop swearing.

KAREEM: Oh, my bad.

Short pause.

MISS: What makes you say that? I should quit? Teaching is… BS?

KAREEM: *(Shrugs.)* Alisha was right, you know. Her speech. You don't really teach us nothin'. Not *you* personally. The system, innit…If all the schools in this country was like dynamited tonight, and all the teachers was wiped out by some horrible plague, I reckon everythin' would be fine in the mornin'. Better even. Your job is bullshit, miss. You should quit. You should go work in a Moroccan spa…No offence.

MISS: No. No offence, Kareem…Maybe I will. In fact, yeah, that's exactly what I'll do. *After* you pass GCSE English.

KAREEM: Ah, I see what you done there, miss –

MISS: In order to achieve that, do you know what is required of you?

Short pause.

KAREEM: *(Shrugs.)* Yeah.

MISS: *(Firmer.)* Do you know what you have to do, Kareem?

KAREEM: Yes, miss. I do.

MISS: Good. See you Friday after school then.

KAREEM: Okay. If you need any more careers advice before then, just ping an email to my secretary.

They look at one another. MISS is unimpressed.

KAREEM: Jokes, miss.

Blackout.

SCENE FIVE

The next day. After school.

MISS sits at the teacher's desk, red pen in hand, marking exercise books again.

JOHN sits on, or leans against, one of the student desks. He is 'smoking' a pen, pretending it's a cigarette, taking long, studied drags, and blowing out luxuriant plumes of invisible smoke.

Silence, until –

MISS: *(Without looking up from her marking.)* I'm ignoring you, John.

JOHN: *(Imitating the students.)* Is it?

MISS: Yes. It is.

JOHN: ...It's Mr Banks to you.

> *Short pause. MISS continues marking. JOHN continues 'smoking'.*

MISS: I'm ignoring you in the hope that you'll go away.

> *Short pause. JOHN doesn't go away.*

MISS: Why are you not going away?

JOHN: *(Again imitating the students.)* Visit, miss, innit.

MISS: Visiting hours are between 'Not now' and 'Fuck off, I'm busy'.

> *Short pause.*

MISS: And yet you're not fucking off.

> *Short pause. She looks up at him.*

JOHN: *(Genuine.)* Don't you just love this school!?!

MISS: John please –

JOHN: *I* do –

MISS: I don't have time for this –

JOHN: I *love* it!

MISS: I have work to do –

JOHN: It's a great fuckin' school. Shall I tell you why?

MISS: No –

JOHN: I walk into any classroom, any time of day, what do I see?

MISS: A cultural vacuum –

JOHN: Children who wanna learn. They wanna learn…Now they're not intelligent. No way. They're not. They're thick as shit. Illiterate. EAL. SEN. ADHD. The lot. *But* they wanna learn. They're *tryin'* to learn. And I love that. I really do. It's a special thing. A glorious thing.

   Short pause.

MISS: Okay –

JOHN: I mean, don't get me wrong. I'm not sayin' we're perfect. We ain't perfect. We got our bad eggs, you know. We do. Not least among the fuckin' staff. Three or four fuckers I'd like to fire right now, if I could…The maths department, for example. Useless cunts. Half of them are fuckin' EAL, let me tell you. Learn the fuckin' language, you lazy bastards. How you gonna to teach trigonometry if you can't even say the fuckin' word? But no – it's a great school. It *is*. An exceptional school. And I *love* it. *But* – And this is my point – *(Continues.)*

MISS: *(Overlaps.)* Oh good –

JOHN: That don't just happen. A school like this don't just chance itself into existence. No. It's teachers like you who *make* it happen. *You* make greatness happen. You do. Every day. You make greatness happen. I want you to remember that –

MISS: John –

JOHN: Remind yourself of it. Say it aloud each morning before you eat your Weetabix –

MISS: John –

JOHN: 'Every day I make greatness happen' –

MISS: John!

JOHN: …Yes.

MISS: …We've been over this…I'm not interested…I don't date other members of staff.

Beat.

JOHN: Who said I…? Now strictly, that's not true, is it, not strictly –

MISS: That was a mistake – a very *short-lived* mistake – and I wish I hadn't told you about it now –

JOHN: No. Okay. Sorry…I didn't mean to…

Short pause.

JOHN: That's not actually why I'm – why I'm here. *Actually.*

MISS: …No?

JOHN: No.

MISS: …Why are you here?

Short pause.

JOHN: I'm, you know, I'm checkin' up. In a professional capacity.

MISS: Checking up on what?

JOHN: …You.

MISS sighs heavily.

JOHN: I worry about you.

MISS: Oh, you as well –

JOHN: I do! What?

MISS: Nothing – I'm fine. You don't need to worry.

JOHN: It's my job to worry. Especially, you know…

MISS: No, John, I don't know. Especially what?

Short pause.

JOHN: Never mind. Just. You seem a bit stressed –

MISS: I'm busy, John! Jesus! I'm busy! In the next hour *(indicates the exercise books)* I've got the Year 11 books to mark, I've a *Jekyll and Hyde* scheme to finish, *and* I've to mount a fucking display for open evening. Which, while I'm doing that, by the way, some union…cunt will materialise out of the wall to tell me to stop, because it's not part of the job description, but what he won't tell me is who the fuck else is going to get it done. That's the next hour, John. All that before I go pick up Rachel. So, yes, I'm busy. I might seem a little stressed. What I don't need is to waste time arguing with you about whether or not I might be about to have a nervous fucking breakdown. Alright?

Short pause.

JOHN: Yes…Alright…Sorry…I wasn't arguing…I was just… engagin' in dialogue. That's all.

Beat.

JOHN: Look, those Year 12 retakes then –

MISS: John, we have had this conversation –

JOHN: Let me help you –

MISS: I don't need your help.

JOHN: You don't? Really? Because you sound pretty fuckin' busy. You sound overrun.

MISS: I am overrun.

JOHN: So let me help.

MISS: You wouldn't be a help, John.

JOHN: ….Of course, I would –

MISS: You're a fucking PE teacher!

JOHN: How difficult can it be?

MISS: You'd just be in the way. Like you're in the way now, John. *You* are stressing me out.

JOHN: Okay. Alright. Fine…

Short pause.

JOHN: All I'm sayin', if you do need help, if you need anything, at all…ask. I'm here.

MISS: I know. I will. Thank you.

JOHN: You're welcome…Right then. I'll leave you to…

MISS: Yes. Please do.

Beat.

JOHN: So that was a no then, was it, regardin' the, eh – us?

MISS: Yes.

JOHN: …Yes, it was a no or –

MISS: It was a no.

JOHN: Okay…

Short pause.

MISS: For now…It was a no for now…

JOHN: …Oh…

Short pause.

MISS: …I like you, John, okay. You know that. I like you. I just – It's very soon after…and I don't know if I have space, at the moment, emotionally, you know. Rachel and school: I think that's all I can manage right now.

JOHN: No, I understand.

MISS: Good…Thank you.

Short pause.

JOHN: *(A joke.)* So you're sayin' there is a chance.

Short pause – MISS is stone-faced.

JOHN: No. Anyway, I'll eh…see you later. Let me know if there's anything I can do. Anything. And remember, 'Every day I make greatness happen…' Do you want to say it with me?

MISS: No, John, I don't want to say it with you.

JOHN: No. Right. Well…Bye then.

MISS: *(Already back to her marking.)* Bye.

JOHN goes. MISS continues marking.

Blackout.

SCENE SIX

The next day. Lunch time.

IMAN is sitting at one of the student desks, notes, pens, highlighters, etc., along with his phone, spread out in front of him. ALISHA is standing up, facing IMAN, almost as if she is the teacher. In her hand, she has a little notebook; now and then she puts it down on the desk and leans over to jot things in it.

ALISHA: Okay, so, *(TV presenter voice)* 'Hello and welcome to the show. I'm your host, Alisha Soneji, and, let me tell you, ladies and gentlemen, we have got some great guests lined up for you tonight –' *(Breaks off.)* I feel like we can do better than 'great'… *Great* guests.

IMAN. Yeah…

Short pause.

IMAN: Oh, why don't we – We could use a, like a power of three…?

ALISHA: …What do you mean?

IMAN: Like uh…I don't know. Uh…'We have some…earth-shattering, mind-blowing…spine-crunching guests for you this evening.'

IMAN looks at ALISHA, desperately hoping for her approval.

ALISHA: *('That's a terrible idea'.)* …Yeah…How about 'special'…? 'We have got some *special* guests lined up for you tonight'?

IMAN: Oh, um…okay, yeah… 'Special'… 'Special' works.

ALISHA: Cool, so, *(faster this time, without the TV voice)* 'Hello and welcome to the show. I'm your host, yadda, yadda. We have got some *special* guests lined up for you tonight –' *(Breaks off.)* Yeah, maybe you're right though. Maybe 'special' is a bit… meh… *(Points to the phone.)* Thesaurus dot com.

IMAN: …Oh, uh –

IMAN picks up his phone.

ALISHA: Look up – Try…'great', I guess.

IMAN: Okay, uhm… *(Types in the letters.)* G-R-A-T – *(Stops, corrects himself.)* E-A-T. 'Great'… Hmm…

Short pause.

IMAN: Well, there's uh, 'ample'? Some 'ample' guests?

ALISHA: No.

IMAN: No…

Short pause – IMAN peruses the online thesaurus.

IMAN: Oh! How 'bout 'peachy'? We have some 'peachy' guests for you tonight?

ALISHA: …Yeah, that's not right either.

IMAN: No, it's not, is it…?

Short pause. More perusing.

IMAN: 'Intrepid'! 'Intrepid guests'!!!

ALISHA: …I think that would mean like they travelled a long way to get here. They had many adventures on their journey. Like Frodo or somethin'.

IMAN: Oh. Yeah. Wait, do you like *Lord of the Rings*?

ALISHA: No! I hate that shit! Ugh, it's so borin'.

IMAN: Oh. Okay –

ALISHA: Why don't we just go with 'excitin''?

IMAN: …Uhm, sure –

ALISHA: 'Excitin'', right? 'Excitin' guests'? That works.

IMAN: I think so?

ALISHA: Definitely. Okay. So, let me – I'm gonna run through the whole thing so far.

IMAN: Cool.

ALISHA: *(Mock dramatic.)* Without notes.

IMAN: Uh, really? Already?

ALISHA: Check this mothafucka out, yo…Ready?

IMAN nods. After a short pause –

ALISHA: *(TV presenter voice.)* 'Hello and welcome to the show. I'm your host, Alisha Soneji, and, let me tell you, ladies and gentlemen, we have got some excitin' guests lined up for you tonight. Their task, as always, is to persuade me, your host, to banish their most hated items to the dreaded Room 101 for all eternity. But it won't be easy, folks. I am feelin' *mean* tonight. *(Strange voice.)* Mean like an evil queen. *(TV presenter voice.)* Well, anyway, let's get on with the show. Can we have a big Room 101 welcome for our first guest? We are so lucky to have him with us this evenin'. All the way from the glitz and glamour of Belmont Circle, ladies and gentlemen, it's my pleasure to introduce to you…Iman… *(Falters.)* Styles –' *(Breaks off.)* Boom! Sorry. I don't know your surname…

Pause – IMAN looks at ALISHA in awe.

IMAN: How do you do that?

ALISHA: …Do what?

IMAN: That. What you just did. It was…Wow – I can't do that.

ALISHA: …Oh –

IMAN: I'm so stupid.

Short pause.

ALISHA: You're not / stupid –

IMAN: I am…I'm dumb…

Short pause.

IMAN: Sorry –

ALISHA: No, it's…Maybe if you just practise more, you know –

IMAN: It's nothing to do with practice. I can't practise having a new brain, can I…? Miss is right. I'm a failure. I shouldn't be here. I'm going to fail again. I know it.

ALISHA: Miss is a fuckin' psycho, dragon bitch, Iman. She like eats children. She traps them in her fuckin' gingerbread house and eats them. You have to take what she said to us and like…use it. Prove her wrong.

IMAN: I can't –

ALISHA: Of course, you can. You just need to like 'Try your best' or whatever.

IMAN: I tried my best last time. I failed.

ALISHA: Okay, but this time you're gonna try even harder. You're gonna make sure you don't fail.

IMAN: That's easy for you to say…You're like a genius.

ALISHA: Iman, I'm not a genius. I failed too, remember.

IMAN: How did you fail? You're…amazing.

ALISHA: I didn't get enough marks. That's how.

IMAN: That doesn't make any sense. If *you* can't pass, Alisha, then I'm…doomed.

ALISHA: I *can* pass, Iman. I'm *going* to pass. It was just, last year…there was like…some stuff going on. In my family. I got…distracted.

IMAN: Oh. Okay…What stuff?

ALISHA: We should get back to work –

IMAN: …Oh. Yeah –

ALISHA: Right. Let's do this, Iman. Come on. We're gonna ace this bitch. Okay?

IMAN: …Okay.

ALISHA: Say it with me.

IMAN: …Uh…?

ALISHA: We gonna ace this bitch!

IMAN: …I'm not / really –

ALISHA: We gonna *ace* this bitch!!!

IMAN: *(Awkward.)* …Uhm…We gonna ace this bitch.

ALISHA: Yeah!

ALISHA looks at IMAN expectantly.

IMAN: *(Still awkward, but with more enthusiasm.)* We gonna ace this bitch!

ALISHA: Fuck yeah! *(A realisation.)* Oh my god, can you imagine if miss walks in and we're here all like 'Yeah! Fuck yeah! We gonna ace this bitch!'

They stop. They turn their eyes toward the door, perhaps leaning forward to peek through the panel of glass. There's no one there. They look at one another again. They explode into laughter.

Blackout.

SCENE SEVEN

The following week.

KAREEM sits alone at one of the desks, laptop open in front of him. He's working!

MISS rockets through the door, carrying her teacher's planner, some exercise books, etc. She stops abruptly.

MISS: Oh. Hi Kareem.

KAREEM: *(Without looking up from the laptop.)* Hi, miss.

> Pause. KAREEM is typing. MISS stares at him. After a moment, KAREEM stops, looks up.

KAREEM: I'm workin'.

MISS: I can see that.

> *Short pause.*

MISS: How does it feel…? Headache? Nausea? Nosebleed?

KAREEM: Ha-ha. Maybe it's comedy you should go into, miss, not like health and beauty.

MISS: Don't start that again. *(Dumps her stuff on the teacher's desk.)* Have you a narrative draft to show me?

KAREEM: …Yeah, about that, see. I been tryin', miss. I swear. It takes time though. You can't rush it. I made bare progress with the…Samantha…?

MISS: The Samantha Brick response.

KAREEM: Yeah, the Samantha Brick thing, and I done like half the narrative. More than half.

MISS: …Okay. Well. Good. I'll take a look at it in a minute. I've got to go deal with some silly Year 9s. Keep working.

KAREEM: Safe, miss.

> *MISS goes to leave.*

KAREEM: The ceilin' is leakin' again, by the way.

MISS: *(As she goes.)* Put the bin under it, would you? I don't
want the floor getting wet.

KAREEM: Okay.

MISS is gone. KAREEM gets up.

KAREEM: *(TV documentary voiceover.)* In between A-level
lessons and preparin' for his GCSE retake exam, Kareem
did janitorial tasks…For his services to the school, he was
presented with a special belt with tools on it and shit.

*KAREEM picks up the bin, looks up at the ceiling, looks down at the
floor, tries to pinpoint exactly where to place the bin. Eventually,
he puts it down. He looks up at the ceiling again. He's satisfied.*

KAREEM: All in a day's work for Kareem, your friendly
caretaker.

*KAREEM sits down again. He focuses on the laptop. After a moment,
a drop of water falls from the ceiling – but it misses the bin. He
looks up from his work.*

KAREEM: *(Addresses the ceiling in an American accent.)* Oh no
you di'n't. *(He gets up.)* You playin' games with me now.
You playin' games, mothafucka. We goan' sort this out
now.

He re-evaluates the situation then moves the bin a little.

KAREEM: *(Still addressing the ceiling.)* Drip again, bitch. I dares
ya. I double dares ya.

He waits. Nothing happens.

KAREEM: Naw, had enough, have ya…? Das right. Ain't
nobody fucks with Kareem, *king* of the caretakers.

*He sits down once more, but this time he's distracted from his work
– he waits for another drop of water to fall. Eventually it does, but
it lands on the floor – in the spot where KAREEM had placed the
bin initially.*

KAREEM: *(Shoots up out of his seat.)* Mothafucka, you tryin' my patience now. In all my years on the job, I ain't never met such a stubborn *(mispronounces the word)* adversarary.

He reassesses the situation – and comes to the conclusion that –

KAREEM: There's two leaks, man. Two fuckin' leaks right there. *(Imitates a burst of static then speaks into an imaginary walkie-talkie.)* 'Calling all premises staff. We got a code blue in sector 19. Over.'

Short pause – he has an idea.

KAREEM: Hold on a minute. Hold on a darn-tootin' minute. Kareem just had hisself an idea. We gots a recyclin' bin. A bigass mothafuckin' recyclin' bin. Much bigger and wider than dis puny bitch normal bin. We goan' switcheroo.

KAREEM swaps the bins, now placing the larger, recycling bin under the ceiling drip (where it will remain for much of the rest of the play). He stands back to admire his work.

KAREEM: And the award goes to…KTam: Kareem Tamam.

Short pause. ALISHA comes in on his next line.

KAREEM: *(Immensely powerful supervillain voice.)* I will not be defeated. Ya hear? I will *not* be defeated.

Short pause. ALISHA scans the room.

ALISHA: …Eh, Kareem –

KAREEM: *(Startled.)* Woah –

ALISHA: Who you talkin' to?

KAREEM: Hey there, Alisha…Eh…The ceilin' drip…I was talkin' to the ceilin' drip…

KAREEM points at the ceiling.

KAREEM: I ended the mothafucka.

ALISHA: …What mothafucka?

KAREEM: The drip…Real nasty sonumbitch.

ALISHA: *('You're weird'.)* Right… *(Takes off her bag, removes notebook, pen, etc.)* Where's miss?

KAREEM: Be back in a minute.

ALISHA: *(Nods.)* …Is there another laptop?

KAREEM: …Eh…I don't think so.

ALISHA: *(Sarcastic.)* Awesome.

Short, awkward pause.

KAREEM: Hey, eh, would you, if you don't mind, would you take a look at my story…? You know, give me a few tips…? You kinda seem like you're good at this stuff.

ALISHA: …Sure. Why not?

KAREEM: Thank you.

They sit down at the laptop.

ALISHA: What's the story about?

KAREEM: …Eh…actually, it's kind of personal…

ALISHA: …Okay…So, do you want me to read it, or –

KAREEM: No, yeah, I do. I do. I just – It's kind of awkward to talk about…

ALISHA: …Ehm…right…

Short pause.

KAREEM: It's about my grandad. He like died. Six weeks ago. It's about the last time I saw him.

ALISHA: …Oh…Fuck…Really?

KAREEM: Yeah.

ALISHA: Woah.

KAREEM: I know… *(Off her look.)* What?

ALISHA: No, nothin'…Nothin'…Sorry to…

KAREEM: Naw. Thank you.

Short, slightly awkward pause.

ALISHA: …So, should I –

KAREEM: Yeah, yeah – Please.

ALISHA nods.

ALISHA: …Right then, eh…

ALISHA starts to read the story, but after about ten seconds, she breaks off –

ALISHA: You're not a fan of the full stop, no?

KAREEM: Fuck no. Don't believe in 'em… *(Off her look.)* Swear down. Full stops. Capital letters. Fuckin' apostrophes. What's the point? You can still read the shit without them, so…

ALISHA: You need to use punctuation, Kareem. If you want to pass the retake, you need to use punctuation.

KAREEM: *(Sighs, then in an American accent.)* Man, y'all be restrictin' my free spirit with your narrow-ass, white man rules.

ALISHA: I ain't restrictin' nothin'. I'm helpin' you get your GCSE, dipshit. Do you even know where the full stops go?

KAREEM: *('No'.)* …Yes.

ALISHA: Go on then…Put them in…

KAREEM: *(Silly voice.)* A'ight…A'ight…Easy now…Let me see here…The full stop go…

Short pause – KAREEM appears to be performing some sort of complex mental calculation, making occasional notes in the air with his index finger.

KAREEM: Carry the two.

Short pause – KAREEM continues to perform this strange routine, until –

ALISHA: *(Reads.)* 'It was dark when she woke me'…

ALISHA looks at KAREEM expectantly…

ALISHA: Full stop.

KAREEM: Full stop, yeah. Exactly.

ALISHA enters a full stop.

ALISHA: *(Reads.)* 'The orange glow from the streetlight outside my bedroom window crept through the crack in the curtains'…

Again, ALISHA looks at KAREEM…

KAREEM: Full stop.

ALISHA: Yes!

ALISHA enters another full stop.

ALISHA: Good boy. You're learnin'.

KAREEM: …'Good boy'…? Did you just say, 'Good boy'?

ALISHA: I did.

KAREEM: I'm not a dog.

ALISHA: No, you're not. A dog could punctuate better than this shit.

KAREEM: What the fuck! You need to watch yo'self, sista –

ALISHA: You actually write nice sentences, Kareem. You just need to like take some care.

KAREEM: Oh, okay, miss. Sorry, miss.

ALISHA: I'm payin' you a compliment, douchebagouche.

KAREEM: It don't sound like no compliment.

ALISHA: Well, it *is*. Do you want me to continue?

KAREEM: *(Grudging.)* …Yes. Please.

ALISHA: Okay, so…?

They read.

KAREEM: Next one after 'hospital', right?

ALISHA: …Yes. That is correct.

She enters another full stop and resumes reading.

ALISHA: *(Without looking away from the screen.)* Were you close with your grandad?

KAREEM: …Yeah…

ALISHA: *(Looks at him.)* …Yeah?

KAREEM: …Yeah.

ALISHA: …You don't wanna like expand on that?

KAREEM: No.

ALISHA: …No. Okay.

She goes back to reading. After a moment –

ALISHA: *(Without looking away from the screen.)* My dad died last year.

KAREEM looks at ALISHA. She continues looking at the laptop.

ALISHA: *(Enters another full stop.)* Full stop.

Short pause.

KAREEM: …Wait, seriously…? Your dad died?

ALISHA: *(Still without looking away from the screen.)* Seriously. My dad died.

KAREEM: …Shit…What happened…? How did he…?

ALISHA: *(Still focused on the laptop.)* He killed himself. In our kitchen. I was the one who like found the body.

Short pause.

KAREEM: …Woah…Fuck –

ALISHA: *(Enters another full stop.)* Full stop.

KAREEM: …Eh, okay, do you think maybe you could ease off on the fuckin' full stops for a minute…?

ALISHA: *(Looks at him.)* …What? I thought you wanted me to –

KAREEM: Yeah, I do, but like, shit, man…This is like…You just…

KAREEM struggles for a moment with the enormity of ALISHA's revelation.

KAREEM: …Are you okay?

ALISHA: *(Looks at the screen again.)* I'm fine.

Short pause.

ALISHA: Most days I'm like…numb. Like it didn't happen almost. But then I get these moments…

Short pause.

ALISHA: Remember the first day, with miss. I was late, and she like destroyed me. In front of you and Iman. She totally humiliated me. The reason I was late – I had a…a moment…like a…a panic attack or something. I locked myself in the toilet. I almost didn't come to – this.

KAREEM: Shit.

ALISHA: And then when I did finally make it, she like shat on my face, literally, and then you were like hittin' on me. And askin' me about my necklace, which, by the way, in answer to your question, it contains some of my dad's ashes.

KAREEM: Oh…Aw, jeez…I feel like such a dick.

ALISHA: It's fine… *(Enters another full stop.)* Full stop.

Short pause.

KAREEM: I wasn't hittin' on you, by the way.

ALISHA: Yes, you were.

KAREEM: No, I wasn't. If I said, gimme your number. Let's go on a date. That would be hittin' on you.

ALISHA: *(Enters an apostrophe.)* Apostrophe.

Beat.

KAREEM: Gimme your number. Let's go on a date.

Short pause.

ALISHA: *(Looks at him.)* Excuse me.

KAREEM: *Now* I'm hittin' on you.

ALISHA: I can see that, you sick fuck.

KAREEM: Come on. Gimme your digits. We should go out.

ALISHA: Why? Because my dad killed himself? Because you get turned on by the thought of a vulnerable, grief-stricken waif in mourning and distress.

KAREEM: No. Yes. I don't know what half that shit means, but, yes, it is kinda turnin' me on.

ALISHA: Eugh, you're disgustin'.

KAREEM: Alisha, I think you're really cool. And also really hot. And I really like you.

ALISHA: …I'm cool *and* hot?

KAREEM: …Yes. See – *that* – that was cool *and* hot. The fact that you said that. The fact that you noticed I said it: cool *and* hot…What do you say?

Short pause.

ALISHA: You got a pen?

KAREEM: No. I never have a pen.

ALISHA: That's a shame…No pen: no digits.

KAREEM: …Wait, for real?

She looks at him – she's serious. He shoots up and scrambles round the room in search of a pen. He picks up a board marker, offers it up for her appraisal.

ALISHA: I said a pen, Kareem.

KAREEM puts the board marker down, exasperated. He searches again.

KAREEM: Can't you just put it in my phone like a normal person – Oh!

He has found a pen. He holds it aloft victoriously.

KAREEM: Pen! Pen!!!!!

He gives her the pen. She sighs. She tries to write her number on the corner of a piece of paper – but the pen doesn't work.

ALISHA: Pen's not workin', Kareem.

KAREEM: Fuck me. *('Gimme the pen'.)* Here.

She gives him the pen. He tries it – but it's still not working.

ALISHA: Maybe it's just not meant to be.

He searches again. He can't find another pen.

KAREEM: It's a school! How can there not be a fuckin' pen?

ALISHA: Hey. Just give me the board marker.

KAREEM: Huh?

ALISHA: The board marker.

He gives her the board marker.

ALISHA: Roll up your sleeve.

He looks at her: 'Are you serious?'

ALISHA: Do you want my number or not? Roll up your sleeve.

He rolls up his sleeve.

ALISHA: Good boy.

She writes her number on his arm.

ALISHA: There you go.

He looks at his arm a moment.

KAREEM: This is your actual number?

ALISHA: Yes.

KAREEM: Your actual telephone number?

ALISHA: Yes!

KAREEM: *(Delighted.)* Alright!

ALISHA: Alright…Don't tell anyone about my dad please.

KAREEM: I won't. I promise.

ALISHA: Good. Thank you. Now, can we get back to your story?

KAREEM: Yes. Absolutely. My story. I love this story. This is my favourite fuckin' story in the whole wide world.

IMAN enters, beset by his humongous school bag.

KAREEM: *(Beams.)* Iman, you buff ting!

IMAN: *(Weirded out.)* …Hey.

ALISHA: 'Sup Iman.

IMAN: …Where's miss?

KAREEM: Be back in a minute.

IMAN: Oh…Okay…Are there any more laptops?

ALISHA: Nope.

IMAN: *(Shrugs.)* Hmm.

IMAN sits down, unpacks his things, sets them out on the desk. He watches ALISHA and KAREEM.

ALISHA: *(Reads.)* 'The roads were empty'…

KAREEM: Full stop.

ALISHA: Indeed, Kareem. Very good –

KAREEM: You see. Me speaks English good –

ALISHA: Maybe you should change the word, 'empty'.

KAREEM: …To…?

ALISHA: *(Dramatic.)* 'Desolate'.

KAREEM: Oooh. Yes. I like it.

ALISHA changes 'empty' to 'desolate'.

IMAN: What're you lots doing?

Short pause.

KAREEM: Alisha's helpin' me with my story.

IMAN: …Oh.

Short pause.

IMAN: Uhm, Alisha, are you still okay to practise our Room 101 stuff today, after the uh –

ALISHA: Huh? Oh. Shit. No. I can't. I gotta look after my little brother.

IMAN: …Oh. Okay.

ALISHA: Sorry.

IMAN: No. That's alright.

Short pause.

IMAN: So, when shall / we –

MISS enters with her usual high – borderline frantic – energy.

MISS: Okay, people, how we getting on? Sorry I got delayed. Year 9 miscreants.

ALISHA: We need laptops, miss.

MISS: Oh, *(almost says 'shit')* shhhoot, are there none…? And no Muhammed either. What a surprise. Iman, would you mind running down to the office? Miss Walker's in there. Just ask her for two laptops please.

IMAN: …Uhm, okay.

IMAN gets up, moves slowly toward the door.

MISS: The recycling bin is your handiwork, Kareem, is it?

KAREEM: Yes, miss. Took real good care of that.

MISS: Thank you. And you're aware, are you, that your arm is covered in board marker?

IMAN stops on his way out. He looks at KAREEM's arm. KAREEM also looks down at his own arm.

KAREEM: What the…? How did that get there…? Alisha, any ideas?

KAREEM and ALISHA look at one another. Beat. They erupt into laughter. IMAN is still watching.

MISS: Okay. Private joke, obviously.

MISS notices IMAN still standing there.

MISS: Iman…? Laptops…

IMAN: …Yes, miss.

IMAN leaves.

MISS: Right, Kareem, you're still working on your story, are you?

KAREEM: Yeah, like, polishing, miss. You know, final touches.

MISS: Okay, so, how 'bout I read a finished draft in…fifteen minutes?

KAREEM: No problem, miss.

MISS: Good. Alisha, anything more to show me –

KAREEM: Let's say twenty minutes, miss. Just to be safe.

MISS: …

KAREEM: Half an hour. Tops.

MISS: …Fine.

KAREEM: Alright. Let me make a note. In my diary here. Mind if I – ?

He takes a pen from MISS.

KAREEM: *(Voices aloud what he's writing in his diary.)* 'Half an hour from now. Give story to favourite teacher'. It's a date, miss. It's a date.

MISS gives KAREEM a friendly shake of the head – she's almost laughing at him. KAREEM winks at ALISHA. ALISHA laughs.

Blackout.

SCENE EIGHT

About forty minutes later.

ALISHA and IMAN are working on their laptops. MISS is standing with KAREEM – she has just finished reading the story from his screen.

MISS: Alright, listen up everybody. Let's pause for a moment…Come on…

Short pause. They all turn their attention to MISS.

MISS: People, something huge has happened here today. Something momentous…In fourteen…whatever, Gutenberg invented the printing press. Five hundred years later, Tim Berners-Lee created *(hesitantly)* the world wide web. And today, October 5th 2016, at this humble state school in old London town, Kareem Tamam completed a story.

ALISHA: Waaaahhhaaa –

KAREEM: Alright.

ALISHA: Miss is parrin' you, man –

KAREEM: Easy now –

MISS: I'm not 'parring' anyone, Alisha. In fact, not only did Kareem complete a story, he completed a good story. A very good story. And thus was heralded a bright new dawn for all humanity –

KAREEM: Woah. Calm down, miss –

ALISHA: What mark would it get?

MISS: Mark, Alisha? What mark, you say…? That there – That right there…with a little more polishing…that's a top band answer –

ALISHA: *(Excitement.)* Owwwww –

KAREEM: Come off it, miss.

MISS: It's true.

KAREEM: Swear down? Top band?

MISS: I swear down, Kareem. I swear right down. Top band. Well done. I'm proud of you –

ALISHA: Congratulations!

KAREEM: *(Award speech.)* Thank you, thank you. This is such an honour. I'd like to thank my manager, my parents, and, most of all, you, my fans. This is for you.

KAREEM is making light of it, but he's genuinely chuffed.

MISS: And let this be a lesson to us all: with a little hard work, we can achieve…

IMAN: Oblivion.

Short pause. Everybody looks at IMAN. Eventually –

KAREEM: Shut up, Iman, you donut –

MISS: Now, children. Play nice, thank you. *(Beat.)* Right everyone, it's *(looks at her watch)* four-thirty. I am going to be here for another hour, at least. If anybody wants to stay, keep working, you're more than welcome.

ALISHA: I have to go, miss.

MISS: That's fine, Alisha. I'm sorry I didn't get a chance to feedback on your narrative today. Come see me tomorrow, would you?

ALISHA: Did you read it?

MISS: Yeah, I did.

ALISHA: Was it good?

MISS: Come chat to me about it tomorrow.

ALISHA: That means no.

MISS: It doesn't mean no. It means come chat to me about it tomorrow. In private.

ALISHA: Alright –

IMAN: I'm leaving too, miss.

MISS: Fine, Iman.

KAREEM: I'll stay, miss.

MISS: Excellent. You're a new man.

KAREEM: Can I just go toilet quickly?

MISS: Yes, of course. Actually, all of you, before you go anywhere, don't forget, Friday after school, we're recording the paired speaking and listening assessments. Be here, on time, please. And be ready this time, all of you. Got that?

ALISHA/KAREEM: *(Together.)* Yes, miss.

MISS: Kareem, I am going to go call Muhammed's parents now. Make sure you have a partner.

KAREEM: Safe, miss.

ALISHA: Bye, miss.

MISS exits. KAREEM walks past ALISHA on his way to the door.

KAREEM: I'll eh *(unsaid: 'be in touch')* –

KAREEM taps his arm with his finger. ALISHA nods.

KAREEM: Thanks for your help.

ALISHA: Any time.

KAREEM exits. IMAN and ALISHA pack up their stuff in silence, but it's clear IMAN wants to say something. Eventually –

IMAN: What's on Kareem's arm?

ALISHA: …Huh?

IMAN: What was written on Kareem's arm?

ALISHA: Oh, eh…I'm not sure.

Short pause. ALISHA continues packing up. IMAN has stopped.

IMAN: It looked like a phone number.

ALISHA: …Did it?

IMAN: Yes.

ALISHA shrugs. Short pause. She continues packing up.

IMAN: Was it your phone number?

Short pause. ALISHA stops. She looks at IMAN.

ALISHA: Is there somethin' you wanna say to me, Iman?

IMAN: …No.

Short pause.

ALISHA: Have you got some sort of problem?

IMAN: …No.

ALISHA: Good. I gotta cut.

IMAN: When are we going to practise our Room 101 again?

Short pause.

ALISHA: Can you do lunchtime tomorrow?

IMAN: …Uh, I have film club.

ALISHA: …What?

IMAN: …Film club…We watch films.

ALISHA: …Okay…Well, I can't do after school, so…

IMAN: Maybe you could come…? To film club.

ALISHA: …How would that work?

IMAN: What do you mean?

ALISHA: If you're watchin' a film, how can you practise?

IMAN: Oh. Yeah.

Short pause.

IMAN: I guess I could skip it. Just this once.

ALISHA: Yeah, that would probably be the best idea.

IMAN: Okay.

ALISHA: I'll see you here then, at lunchtime.

IMAN: Sure.

ALISHA nods. She's about to leave.

IMAN: You could come another time…? To film club…It's really cool. We watch films, and like…talk…about…films.

ALISHA: …Yeah…I'm not that into films, Iman. Not my thing.

IMAN: …Oh –

ALISHA: Anyway, I really need to go, so…

IMAN: Okay. I'll see you tomorrow then.

ALISHA: Yeah. Bye, Iman.

IMAN: Bye.

ALISHA leaves. IMAN looks down at the floor, dejected. Beat. He looks up. He stares at KAREEM's laptop. Beat. IMAN walks slowly toward the laptop. He stops. He looks at the screen. A Word document is open – it's KAREEM's story. Beat. IMAN moves toward the door and looks through the panel of glass – there's no one coming. He goes back to the laptop. He selects everything in the document bar, the title, then he presses delete. He closes the document, then opens it up again. He walks back to his desk and continues packing up.

MISS returns. She smiles at IMAN. He smiles back and finishes packing up while MISS sits down at the teacher's desk.

IMAN: Bye, miss.

MISS: Bye, Iman. Well done today.

IMAN: Thanks, miss.

IMAN leaves. MISS starts to tap away at the desktop keyboard, gently humming a jolly tune as she does so. KAREEM enters –

KAREEM: *(Sings Miley Cyrus.)* 'I came in like a wrecking ball'.

MISS: *(Sings Bruce Springsteen.)* 'Bring on your wrecking ball'.

KAREEM: Yeah, that's not how it goes, miss. Also, please never sing again *(trails off in the middle of 'again')* –

KAREEM has noticed the empty document on the laptop. He spends a moment or two trying to locate the story. He can't find it.

KAREEM: Miss…?

MISS: *(Focused on her work.)* …Uh-huh…?

KAREEM: …My work is gone.

MISS: Very funny, Kareem.

KAREEM: I'm serious. My story's gone.

Short pause – MISS looks up from her computer: 'You're joking'.

KAREEM: For real, miss. The document's empty. I can't find it.

MISS: *(Sighs.)* …These computers are useless. You saved a copy, right?

KAREEM: Yeah, of course I did. Of course I saved it, but it ain't there, miss. It's gone. *(Beat.)* Who was in here when you got back? Just now. Was there anyone here?

MISS: *(Nods.)* …Iman.

KAREEM: …On his own?

MISS: Yes.

KAREEM: …Little fuckin' / prick –

MISS: Kareem! Language. Please…Are you suggesting Iman deleted your story?

KAREEM: No, miss, I ain't suggesting nothin'. I'm saying it for sure. Iman deleted my story. It weren't no dodgy computer. It was him. *(Slams the laptop shut.)* Fuck, man.

KAREEM thunders out of the room.

MISS: Kareem…

MISS is alone.

BLACKOUT.

Act Two

SCENE NINE

The next day. Early morning.

MISS is sitting at the desktop computer. JOHN stands before her.

JOHN: Michael Gove. Michael fuckin' Gove. Say what you like about him. I mean, yes, he's a cunt. An ugly cunt. Looks like an under-evolved, deep sea proto-fish. But he was right. The man was right. About one thing, anyway. Coursework. Controlled assessments. Get rid. Get fuckin' rid. Save us all a fuckload of hassle. Now, if he'd done away with a few other things, say, Ofsted, or PSHE, *then /* you'd see –

MISS: John.

JOHN: …Yes.

MISS: Have you resolved anything?

JOHN: Have I fuck…? Iman denies it. Alisha denies it. Neither of 'em saw…whatever there was to see. If anything. There's no evidence. Beyond a story that ain't there. Who fuckin' knows what happened? Not me. And IT can't retrieve it neither.

MISS: …Okay…So…?

JOHN: So, Kareem writes the thing again, don't he?

MISS: Right. And you've said this to him?

JOHN: Yeah, course, I have. Course, I have. He's a good lad: Kareem. He calmed down quick enough. He'll get on with it now, no problem. Case closed. On we plod.

MISS: *(Not convinced.)* Mmm.

JOHN: If there's any more trouble, you know where I am.

MISS: I do, yes. Thank you. I appreciate your help.

JOHN: That's okay. No problem. Or in this instance, no solution. But anyway, yeah…Not to worry…Not to worry…

Short, slightly awkward pause. MISS waits for JOHN to leave, but he doesn't leave.

JOHN: You alright then, otherwise?

MISS: Yes. Yeah.

JOHN: Good…Great…Excellent…

Another short, awkward pause.

JOHN: How's Rachel?

MISS: Rachel's fine.

JOHN: Great…Lovely…Lovely…Yeah – She sees, eh, she sees James, does she, on a / regular –

MISS: I'd really prefer not to have this conversation now, John –

JOHN: Oh. No. Sorry. I eh – No, you're right. Sorry…Mind my own…Yep…

Another short, even more awkward pause.

JOHN: Nah, I was just – I was wonderin' really, if eh, you know, if you managed to free up some of that emotional space you mentioned? Any room now for a bit of… romance?

Short pause.

MISS: It's been a week, John.

JOHN: …Has it?

MISS: Yes. A week ago today since you last propositioned me in the workplace.

JOHN: …Oh…Okay…Not sure I like that term: propositioned in the, eh…Do you keep a, like a record –

MISS: No, John, I don't keep a record. I remember.

JOHN: Ah…I see…I see…Well, maybe a little more time then…

Another short, awkward pause.

JOHN: Not goin' anywhere, am I…? Except now…Now I *am* goin' somewhere…Back to my office. To do…stuff. Important head of sixth form stuff –

MISS: Bye, John. Thank you, again.

JOHN: Pleasure.

After a short pause, JOHN leaves. MISS stares at her computer screen. Blackout.

SCENE TEN

A few hours later. Lunchtime.

IMAN sits alone at one of the desks. He checks the time. He waits. Eventually…

ALISHA arrives.

IMAN: Oh, hey, I thought you forgot –

ALISHA: Why d'you delete Kareem's story?

IMAN: …What?

ALISHA: Kareem's story. You deleted it. I want to know why.

IMAN: …How do you know I deleted it?

ALISHA: Kareem told me.

IMAN: How?

ALISHA: …How what?

IMAN: How did he tell you?

ALISHA: The fuck does it matter how he told me…? You deleted his fuckin' coursework!

IMAN: …You gave him your number, didn't you?

ALISHA: …Oh my god. Oh my god. You're a fuckin' freak.

IMAN: I'm not a freak.

ALISHA: Well, what the fuck is wrong with you then? What kind of horrible cunt deletes someone else's coursework…? How could you do that to Kareem –

IMAN: Kareem's a bully, alright. He's a bully. That's why I did it. Bullies don't deserve to do well –

ALISHA: He's not a bully. How is he a bully?

IMAN: Five years, that's how. Every day for the last five years he's been telling me how he fucks my mum, how she loves him more than me, cos he fucks her so good, how soon he's gonna be my stepdad. He knows I never had a dad. He knows that. He says it deliberately. To be cruel. He's a bully.

Beat.

ALISHA: Kareem says that?

IMAN: Yes. Like every time he sees me.

Short pause.

ALISHA: Oh…I didn't know…

IMAN: Yeah, well…

Short pause.

ALISHA: That ain't cool…I'm sorry.

Beat.

ALISHA: Look, Iman, that don't change nothin'. You deleted his coursework. You need to own up to it.

IMAN: I'm not owning up to anything.

ALISHA: Iman, if you don't fess up, I'm gonna tell miss. You just admitted it to me. I'm gonna tell her.

IMAN: No, you're not.

ALISHA: Eh, yes, I am.

IMAN: You tell miss how I deleted Kareem's work, I'll tell her how you helped him write it – you cheated.

ALISHA: …I never cheated.

IMAN: I saw you yesterday, Alisha.

ALISHA: What did you see?

IMAN: You wrote half the story for him.

ALISHA: …I told him where to put a few fuckin' full stops. That's all. That's not cheatin'.

IMAN: You told him what words to use.

ALISHA: Like, one time, one word –

IMAN: You cheated. You cheated together –

ALISHA: Oh my days, man –

IMAN: Cheating is worse than deleting. Cheating – you could get disqualified. If you get caught.

ALISHA: This is blackmail, Iman. You're fuckin' blackmailin' me –

IMAN: I'm protecting myself. You should protect yourself too. You already failed once –

ALISHA: Fuck you. You know what – *(Right up in his face.)* Fuck. You.

IMAN: We need to practise, Alisha.

ALISHA: No, we don't need to practise. We ain't never practisin' again. As soon as this Room 101 bullshit is over, I don't want nothin' more to do with you. Ever.

IMAN: Can I have your phone number?

ALISHA: *(Utter disbelief.)* …What?

IMAN: If you give me your number, we can practise over the phone.

ALISHA: Are you retarded, Iman? Seriously. Are you on the SEN register?

IMAN: …Yes, actually, I am on the SEN register, and I'm quite sensitive about it.

ALISHA: Boo-fuckin'-hoo, bitch. I'm so sorry for you. I tell you what. Why don't I give you my number then? It's 075-stay-the-fuck-away-from-me-freak.

As ALISHA goes to exit, she meets KAREEM on his way in.

KAREEM: *(Addressing IMAN.)* Well, look who it is –

ALISHA: We're leavin', Kareem.

KAREEM: Leavin'? I just arrived. I ain't goin' nowhere. Not until I get some answers. Why d'you delete my story, Iman? Why d'you delete my fuckin' story, you pathetic little cunt hair?

IMAN: I didn't delete your story. Did I, Alisha?

ALISHA: Kareem, let's go –

IMAN: You probably deleted it yourself, idiot.

KAREEM: Oh, I deleted it myself, did I? Yeah. How 'bout I fuckin' delete you, Iman? How 'bout I smash your fuckin' faggoty little head in –

ALISHA: Oh, great, Kareem. Great idea. Kick his head in. Get yourself excluded for this fuckin' wasteman. Come on. He ain't worth the trouble.

KAREEM: Naw, ain't no trouble, Alisha. Ain't no trouble. I'm gonna enjoy it. I'm gonna love fuckin' this pussy ass bitch right up –

IMAN: *(Backing away.)* Come on then, yeah –

KAREEM: Oh, I'm comin' –

ALISHA: Kareem –

As KAREEM advances on IMAN, MISS arrives. Everyone stops. They all look at MISS. Beat.

MISS: What's going on?

Short pause.

KAREEM: Nothin', miss. We was just havin' a vigorous debate.

Short pause.

MISS: A debate?

KAREEM: Yeah. The topic was what should happen to backstabbin', two-faced, little snakes?

MISS: Kareem, Mr Banks has dealt with this already –

KAREEM: Banks didn't deal with shit.

MISS: Don't swear at me! Okay! Do not swear at me!!!

Short pause.

MISS: Mr Banks has dealt with the issue. Now you need to move on –

KAREEM: What punishment did Iman get?

MISS: He didn't delete the story, Kareem. Why would there be a punishment? There was no crime. Iman, did you delete the story?

IMAN: No. I already told Mr Banks –

MISS: There you go, Kareem. He didn't delete it.

Short pause – KAREEM shakes his head. He looks to ALISHA to back him up. She looks away.

KAREEM: He's lyin'.

MISS: That's not for you to decide –

KAREEM: He's lyin', and if Banks won't do nothin' about it –

MISS: What? You're going to sort him out, are you? You're going to beat him up?

KAREEM: Yeah, I am.

MISS: Kareem, you lay one finger on Iman, you will be permanently excluded from this school, but that will be the least of your problems, because you will also have to justify your behaviour to the police. Now, I have work to do. And so do you, Kareem. Go rewrite your story. Alisha, I need to talk to you a minute please.

Short pause – no one moves.

MISS: Now, Kareem! Go!

KAREEM: This ain't finished yet, freshie –

MISS: Did you not hear what I just said? This is the end of it! *Over. Finito.* Now get out of here!

KAREEM leaves. ALISHA waits for MISS. MISS turns to look at IMAN. Then ALISHA turns to look at IMAN. Short pause.

IMAN: …I'm just waiting a minute. For him to…

MISS nods. An awkward pause – then IMAN goes to the door, looks out, but before he leaves, he sticks his head back in –

IMAN: Uhm, Alisha, about our practice –

ALISHA: There is no 'our practice' –

IMAN: …Uhm –

ALISHA: Miss needs to talk to me, Iman. Bye.

Short pause.

IMAN: Bye then. I'll catch you later.

ALISHA. *(To herself.)* No, you won't.

IMAN goes.

ALISHA: *(With a hint of petulance.)* Yes?

MISS: What was that about?

ALISHA: Did you wanna talk to me, or…?

MISS: Yes. I do.

Short pause.

MISS: I read your story.

ALISHA: Okay.

Short pause.

MISS: I can't let you use it, I'm afraid.

ALISHA: …What? Why not?

MISS: …The exam board – they're really clear. They don't like stories that are violent or improbable.

ALISHA: Improbable?

MISS: …Unrealistic.

ALISHA: It's not unrealistic. It happened to me.

MISS: …Sorry?

ALISHA: You told me to write a personal story. This is *my* personal story –

MISS: Wait, hang on, this – it happened to you?

ALISHA: Yes, that's what I just said, isn't it?

MISS: …Does the school know – does Mr Banks know?

ALISHA: O' course they know. That's why I'm here, innit. It weren't no mistake. Not for me. They let me in because *(unsaid: 'my dad killed himself')*…

MISS: …Right. I see. That's…Look, that doesn't change anything…I still can't let you use it.

ALISHA: Why not?

MISS: I just told you why. / It's too –

ALISHA: Is it not a good story?

MISS: No, it is. It's a great story. It's brilliantly written –

ALISHA: So why can't I use it then?

74

MISS: Because those are the rules, Alisha. Those are the rules. It's frustrating, I know, but that's – the story's too violent. The exam board won't accept it. You're going to have to do another one. You're going to have to write a different story.

Beat.

ALISHA: This is bullshit, man!

MISS: …Excuse me?

ALISHA: It's bullshit! *You* are bullshit! Banks is bullshit! The whole school. All of you. The exam. Everythin'. It's bullshit!

Short pause.

MISS: Okay, well, thank you for that, Alisha. I'm really enjoying the retake process too. I wish I could devote more time to it. Instead of, you know, running the English department. Which is my actual job. Hey ho. Life sucks. But let's get on with it. *Do the story again –*

ALISHA: You really hate your life, don't you? I'd feel sorry for you, if you weren't such a bitter fuckin' bitch.

ALISHA storms out. MISS is stunned.

Blackout.

SCENE ELEVEN

The next day.

IMAN, KAREEM, and ALISHA are dotted across the classroom, sitting apart from one another. MISS is perched on one of the student desks at the head of the room, her feet resting on a chair.

Silence. Waiting. Simmering displeasure. More waiting. Eventually –

KAREEM: He ain't gonna show, miss.

MISS: I spoke to his father on Wednesday, Kareem. He said he'd be here.

KAREEM: I know that, miss. You said. Like seven times. But look around. No Muhammed. He ain't gonna show. He never shows.

MISS: Just give it another minute please.

IMAN: Miss, can *we (meaning IMAN and ALISHA)* go at least…?

MISS: No.

IMAN sighs heavily. More silence. More waiting.

KAREEM: He ain't comin', miss.

MISS: Give it another minute. Please.

More silence. More waiting.

IMAN: Miss, I don't understand why *we* can't go –

MISS: Jesus Christ –

IMAN: We already did ours –

ALISHA: She asked us to stay, Iman, okay? That's why. Now stop whinin'.

MISS: One more minute, alright.

IMAN sighs heavily again. Short pause.

IMAN: *(Barely audible.)* I'm not whining. I'm just asking a question.

More silence. More waiting.

KAREEM: Miss, seriously, he ain't comin' –

MISS: Okay, he's not coming! You're right! The boy is not coming! Which is why I asked you and Alisha to stay, Iman. Muhammed is obviously not…reliable. Is he retaking the exam? Does he even exist? He sends me his coursework, but is it really his coursework? Who knows? The point is I think we need to find a new partner for Kareem…Someone else is going to have to step up…

Short pause.

KAREEM: I ain't workin' with Iman, miss –

IMAN: I'm not working with Kareem –

MISS: Well, that kind of narrows the options then, doesn't it?

All eyes turn to ALISHA. Short pause.

ALISHA: When, miss? Like now?

MISS: *(Shakes her head.)* …Next week. You could prepare it over the weekend maybe? And we could do it in Wednesday's session. That's probably the latest we can push it…What do you say…?

ALISHA: Sure.

IMAN turns away, his relief that he doesn't have to work with KAREEM quickly turning to jealousy that KAREEM gets to work with ALISHA. IMAN closes his eyes.

MISS: You'll do it?

ALISHA: Yeah. No problem.

MISS: Thank you.

KAREEM: Safe, Alisha –

MISS: Okay. Good. That's one little obstacle surmounted. Iman, *now* you can go. All of you, in fact. Be gone.

KAREEM and ALISHA stand up. IMAN remains seated, eyes closed. One by one, the others notice him, until eventually everyone is staring at IMAN.

MISS: Iman…?

No response.

MISS: Iman…?

Short pause. MISS gestures to the others silently: 'What's going on?' Another short pause and then – IMAN bolts up out of his seat and walks quickly out the door without a word to anyone. They look at each other, confused.

KAREEM: Anyway –

ALISHA: *(Sing-song.)* Weirdo.

MISS: …Anyone know what that was about?

KAREEM and ALISHA shake their heads, shrug.

KAREEM: *(Points to the door.)* Are you –

ALISHA: *(Nods.)* One second. Wait for me.

KAREEM nods, exits. ALISHA approaches MISS tentatively.

MISS: *(Faux friendly.)* Alisha, how can I help you?

ALISHA: *(Hands MISS a document.)* I wrote another story.

MISS: …That was quick.

ALISHA: …Didn't have much choice, did I…?

MISS: No, you didn't.

ALISHA: It's about people drinkin' tea and goin' Morrison's and other realistic events.

MISS: *(Sarcasm.)* Sounds great.

Short pause.

MISS: I'll mark it over the weekend.

ALISHA: …Safe, miss…Am I in trouble…? For yesterday…?

Short pause.

MISS: I haven't told Mr Banks, if that's what you mean.

ALISHA: …Thank you.

MISS: You're welcome…

Short pause.

MISS: I'm sorry about your…what happened your *(unsaid: 'father')…*

ALISHA nods.

ALISHA: See you next week.

MISS: Next week.

ALISHA goes.

Blackout.

SCENE TWELVE

The following week.

KAREEM paces back and forth slowly across the classroom in silence. He's trying to think of something. ALISHA is sitting at one of the desks. She's thinking too. She stops – takes out her phone.

KAREEM: Oi. Phone away. Focus.

ALISHA: *(Sighs.)* …I'm bored.

KAREEM: No, you're not. One more item. Come on.

ALISHA: Alright. My bad.

She puts her phone away. KAREEM starts to pace again. After a few seconds –

ALISHA: Do you think miss is married?

KAREEM: *(Turns to her.)* …Room 101. Stay focused.

ALISHA: Okay, okay…I'm thinkin'.

KAREEM paces again. After a few more seconds –

KAREEM: She *is* quite fit.

ALISHA: …She's like…fifty!

KAREEM: …So?

ALISHA: Eeew. Gross.

KAREEM: *(Barry White voice.)* It's only natural, baby.

ALISHA: You're disgustin'.

Short pause.

KAREEM: Ain't just me. Mr Banks has a major boner for her.

ALISHA: Kareem!

KAREEM: He does, man –

ALISHA: Stop it. I'm gonna spew, blad. I'm like visualising his boner.

KAREEM: Oh my god, man!

ALISHA: Exactly.

KAREEM turns away, horrified, paces some more. After a pause –

ALISHA: That ain't what I asked.

KAREEM looks at ALISHA, shrugs: he doesn't know if MISS is married. He continues pacing. After another few seconds –

KAREEM: Do you wanna get married?

ALISHA: …Eh, did you just propose?

KAREEM: No! When you're older, I mean.

ALISHA: I know what you mean. I'm gassin'.

Short pause.

ALISHA: Naw, I'm like against marriage.

KAREEM: …Why?

ALISHA: …I'm a feminist, innit.

KAREEM pulls a face.

ALISHA: Maybe you could put marriage into Room 101?

KAREEM: *(Pulls a face again.)* …Das gay.

ALISHA: …Why?

KAREEM: Because it is. I ain't no homophone, yeah. But that is pure gayness.

ALISHA: Homopho*b*e, idiot.

KAREEM: …That's what I said.

ALISHA: You said 'homopho*ne*'. Like 'there' and 'their'.

KAREEM: …The fuck you chattin' about? There and there?

ALISHA: *(Waves a dismissive hand.)* …Nothin'…You come up with a better idea then.

KAREEM: I am. I'm tryin'. *(Taps his head.)* I'm thinkin'…The wheels are startin' to…revolve, innit.

ALISHA: Yeah, that's some real fast fuckin' revolvin' there, Kareem. Slow down. Somebody gonna get hurt. So many ideas. Flyin' around like bullets –

KAREEM: Alright…Alright…

ALISHA smiles. Beat.

ALISHA: Did you know Iman's dad is not around?

KAREEM: …Huh?

ALISHA: Iman – he don't see his dad.

KAREEM: …Oh. Okay.

ALISHA: Did you know?

KAREEM: No. We ain't exactly BFFs.

ALISHA: Nah.

Short pause.

ALISHA: He said you make jokes all the time about fuckin' his mum and how you're gonna become his stepdad.

KAREEM: …What?

ALISHA: That's what he said.

KAREEM: Oh my days.

KAREEM sighs, shakes his head.

ALISHA: It's not true?

KAREEM: No. I never said nothin' about his mum, or his stepdad, or whatever. The guy is *(taps his head again)* diseased, man. He ain't right.

ALISHA: …Why would he make that up though?

KAREEM: Because, yeah. He's messed up. That's why. He tells lies. I fucked his mum! Jeez!

ALISHA: …She not old enough for you?

KAREEM: *(Deadpan.)* …LOL.

ALISHA: *(Suddenly an idea.)* Liars! You should put liars in Room 101!

KAREEM: I should?

ALISHA: Yes! We're doin' it on Wednesday, right? Iman will be there. He'll be watchin'. So we'll make it about liars. We'll make it about him. Not like directly. We ain't gonna say his name, but he'll know, and miss'll know, and it'll be like – fuck you!!!

KAREEM: …You are like a genius, girl!

ALISHA: I am. I know –

KAREEM: An evil genius. You're givin' *me* a boner.

ALISHA: Kareem!

KAREEM: Sorry…You are though. I wanna kiss you.

Short pause.

ALISHA: Do you?

KAREEM: Yes. I really do.

Short pause.

ALISHA: What a shame we're so busy. 'Stay focused', remember?

KAREEM: Awww. Now she's usin' my own words to torment me. This woman is cruel.

ALISHA: Yes, she is.

ALISHA smiles ironically. Short pause.

ALISHA: I suppose she could use a break though.

KAREEM: Oh, she could, she really could –

ALISHA: Just a short one.

KAREEM: Or a long one even…

ALISHA: A long one?

KAREEM: Real long, know what I'm saying?

ALISHA shakes her head, laughs. Beat. They kiss. When they break off –

ALISHA: Wow! I changed my mind. Let's get married.

KAREEM: Okay. Cool. Just gimme like fifteen years.

ALISHA: I ain't waitin' fifteen years. Now or never, fam.

KAREEM: Never then. Too bad.

ALISHA: Yeah, it is too bad. That's the last time I help you with your school work.

KAREEM: Oh, that's sad, cos I was kinda hopin' you might wanna do my other coursework pieces for me…

Short pause. ALISHA looks at him: 'Are you serious?'

KAREEM: For real, Alisha, I don't wanna fail again.

ALISHA: …You're not gonna fail. You done a wicked story.

KAREEM: Not by myself though. I need your help. Seriously. I like started them already. Both of them. They just need, you know, some fixin'. Some of that queen Alisha magic.

ALISHA: You're askin' me to cheat, Kareem.

KAREEM: I'm *(mispronounces the word)* aksin' you to help me. Make sure I don't fail. I can't fail again, man. My dad will like…end me. I can't fail.

Short pause.

ALISHA: Fine. Send them to me.

KAREEM: …Really?

ALISHA: Yeah, whatever, it don't mean nothin' anyway. It's all bullshit –

KAREEM: Safe, Alisha, you are like the bestest, most fittest, most sexiest queen lady –

ALISHA: Okay, alright, calm down. You can repay me with a kiss. Then let's get back to this Room 101 shit.

KAREEM: Yes, your majesty.

They kiss again.

Blackout.

SCENE THIRTEEN

Two days later.

IMAN is sitting at a desk at the front of the room, laptop open in front of him. IMAN's bag is under a desk near the back of the room. His things – pencil case, notepad, etc. – are set out neatly on this desk. MISS is standing with IMAN, reading the work on his screen. The bin is still positioned beneath the ceiling leak.

After a short silence –

MISS: It doesn't make any sense, Iman.

IMAN: …Oh.

MISS: What are trying to say? What point are you trying to make?

IMAN: …

MISS: Your best bet, either start the paragraph again, or scrap it –

KAREEM and ALISHA come through the door, smiling, laughing. KAREEM has some papers in his hand. MISS looks up, unimpressed. They stop.

KAREEM: Miss, I can explain –

MISS: You're late –

KAREEM: Miss, it's okay –

MISS: What did I say about being on time?

KAREEM: I was printin' my coursework, miss. It's finished. All three pieces. Completely done. See? *(Sets the work down on one of the desks.)* One potata. Two potata. Three potatas. *And (waves another piece of paper at her)* Room 101, all ready to go. *(Semi-ironic.)* What I need now, miss, is praise, not punishment.

After a short pause, MISS picks the work up off the desk. She scans through it for a moment, stone-faced, then she looks at ALISHA.

MISS: What's your excuse?

KAREEM: She was helpin' me, miss. See, I'm banned from printin'. There was a incident last month. The librarian – I was falsely accused, yeah. It was very traumatic. I'd rather not go into the details. Anyways, I had to print off of Alisha's account, see. She very kindly agreed to assist me. She too deserves praise.

Short pause.

MISS: Is this all true, Alisha?

ALISHA: Yes, miss.

Short pause.

MISS: You should have told me beforehand, Kareem. That would've been polite.

KAREEM: I know, miss. I'm sorry. It's just – it all happened so fast. The coursework, it came to me. From above. From God. God sent it me. And we was practisin'. Like 24-7. There just wasn't no time. If only there was more time –

MISS: Okay, Kareem. Okay. I get the picture…You're ready for the speaking and listening?

KAREEM: Absolutely. Well, almost. *(Indicates the sheet of paper again.)* Can I just have like five minutes to look over this?

MISS: …Yes. Fine. *(Sits down.)* I can start marking your work while you do that – *(Continues.)*

KAREEM and ALISHA sit down. ALISHA takes out her notebook, starts reading.

MISS: *(Remembers.)* Ah *(almost says 'shit')* shhh-ugar. I've left the recorder in the office. Iman, would you mind running out?

IMAN: *('Again?')* …Uhm, okay.

MISS: Here, take my keys in case it's locked. The recorders are in a box at the bottom of the tall cabinet on the left-hand side of the room.

IMAN: Tall cabinet. Left-hand side.

MISS: You got it?

IMAN: I think so.

MISS: Good man. Thank you. Be quick please.

MISS starts to read KAREEM's work.

KAREEM: Here, I need a pen. *(Gets up.)* Iman, gimme a pen, bruv. Is that your stuff?

KAREEM walks down to the desk with IMAN's stuff on it, picks up IMAN's pencil case.

IMAN: Leave my pencil case alone.

KAREEM: I just need to borrow a pen, man.

ALISHA: You can have mine, Kareem.

IMAN takes his pencil case from KAREEM, picks up his bag, puts the pencil case away, and leaves, taking the bag with him.

KAREEM: *(Sarcasm.)* Thanks, mate.

ALISHA: *(Offers him her pen.)* Kareem…

KAREEM: *(Takes the pen.)* Safe, Alisha. Team, yeah. *Team Kareem.*

KAREEM sits down.

ALISHA: *Team Don't Lose My Pen.*

KAREEM: *Team Watch Your Mouth, Girl, or I'll Slap You Up –*

MISS: *(Without looking up from her reading.)* Kareem, are you looking over your notes, or…what're you doing?

KAREEM: Sorry, miss. She's distractin' me. Bad influence.

MISS looks up, eyeballs KAREEM.

KAREEM: *(A more genuine apology.)* Sorry, miss.

He points at the notes, nods, gives MISS a thumbs-up. He starts to read his notes. MISS goes back to her reading. A moment of silence – maybe ten seconds. Then ALISHA coughs gently or sniffs or clears her throat. KAREEM turns to ALISHA with his finger on his lips and does a very quiet, 'Shhh.' ALISHA shakes her head, stifles a laugh. Then –

ALISHA: We should practise this out loud, Kareem.

KAREEM: Nah, just like, I need to write some stuff on the sheet first, innit.

ALISHA: Why, man? How's that gonna help?

KAREEM: Shut up and let me work, yeah –

MISS: *(Looks up again.)* This is really good, Kareem: your persuasive piece.

KAREEM: Oh. Why, thank you, miss. How sweet of you to say.

MISS: No, honestly. I'm really impressed.

KAREEM: Okay, miss. Just be careful. Alisha be gettin' jealous.

MISS: It's not *that* good, Kareem. You still have a way to go before you reach Alisha standard.

ALISHA: …Did you read my new story, miss?

MISS: I did…

ALISHA looks at MISS in expectation of a verdict…

MISS: It's great.

ALISHA: *(Smiles.)* Thank you. What mark would it get, miss?

IMAN returns.

IMAN: Miss, there's no recorders.

MISS: …Seriously?

IMAN: I found the box, but it was empty.

MISS: Were there no teachers in the office?

IMAN: No, miss.

MISS: They never bring the bloody recorders back. *(Sighs.)* Did you check the sign-out sheet…?

IMAN: …

MISS: On the wall beside the cabinet?

IMAN: …Uh…No…I didn't know there was a sign-out sheet –

KAREEM: Miss, why don't we just use my phone?

MISS: *(Shakes her head.)* I'll run out to the office. Just give me a minute.

KAREEM: Safe, miss. No stress.

IMAN: Your keys, miss –

MISS: Thank you.

MISS goes out.

KAREEM: You should've checked the sign-out sheet, Iman. Schoolboy error.

IMAN ignores KAREEM. He takes his bag off and sits down again.

ALISHA: Kareem, come on, let's practise it out loud.

KAREEM: I need to make some notes first, fam.

ALISHA sighs. KAREEM goes back to his notes. He tries to write something on his sheet. The pen doesn't work. He tries again. He gives up.

KAREEM: Your pen don't work.

ALISHA: Okay, so can we just practise it then / please –

KAREEM: *(Gets up.)* Oi, Iman, I need a pen.

IMAN: I'm not giving you a pen.

> KAREEM goes over to IMAN.

KAREEM: Come on, freshie. Gimme a pen.

IMAN: No.

ALISHA: Kareem –

KAREEM: Gimme a pen –

ALISHA: He doesn't wanna give you a pen.

KAREEM: Gimme a fuckin' pen, dickwad.

IMAN: I said no –

ALISHA: Kareem –

KAREEM: I said yes.

> KAREEM snatches IMAN's bag and quickly moves away.

IMAN: Hey, give that back –

ALISHA: Kareem, come on, miss'll be back in a minute –

KAREEM: I'm just gettin' a pen, yeah –

IMAN: Gimme my bag.

KAREEM: Ooh, Iman's all demandin' and shit –

ALISHA: Kareem, you're bein' an idiot. We need to practise –

IMAN: *Give me my bag, now.*

> Short pause.

KAREEM: Or what…? What you gonna do?

> After a short pause, IMAN tries to grab the bag, but KAREEM moves out of the way.

ALISHA: Kareem –

IMAN: Give me my bag.

KAREEM: No –

ALISHA: That's bait, man –

IMAN: I said, give it to me –

IMAN lunges for the bag, but again KAREEM evades him.

KAREEM: Aw, I like this game, don't you? Take your bag back, Iman. Take it back. Come on. Take it back, boy.

ALISHA: Kareem –

IMAN goes for the bag once more, but again he misses.

KAREEM: Oooh, not havin' so much luck. Wanna try again? Wanna try again, faggot?

IMAN: *(A cry of pure rage.)* FUCK YOU!

IMAN charges at KAREEM who sidesteps and sticks out a foot, bringing IMAN crashing to the floor.

ALISHA: Kareem! Oh my god!

ALISHA rushes to IMAN.

ALISHA: Are you okay?

KAREEM: He's fine. Ain't you, Iman? *(Opens the bag.)* Hey, uh, mind if I borrow a pen?

IMAN: *(On the floor.)* Stay out of my bag.

KAREEM rummages in the bag. Beat. His hand emerges holding an audio recorder. An incredulous pause before –

KAREEM: The bag is full of recorders.

ALISHA: …What?

KAREEM: There's like four fuckin' recorders in here, look… He stole them…He teefed the recorders.

ALISHA: Iman, what the fuck –

KAREEM: I can't believe this shit –

IMAN: Stay out of my bag –

ALISHA: Why would you…?

Beat.

KAREEM: To stop me doin' my fuckin' assessment, innit. He's been fuckin' with me the whole time. First, the story. Now, this. Now, the fuckin' recorders. Fuck, man. I am gonna fuck you up –

ALISHA: Kareem –

KAREEM advances on IMAN who sees him coming, yelps, and tries to crawl away along the floor. As this is happening, ALISHA steps into KAREEM's path, making her body a barrier between the two boys.

KAREEM: Get out the way.

ALISHA: Back off and calm down.

KAREEM: Get out the fuckin' way, Alisha. I'm serious.

ALISHA: *I*'m fuckin' serious. Nobody is havin' a fight here, okay.

KAREEM: Alisha, swear down, if you don't get out the way, I will fuckin'…

ALISHA: What, Kareem…? You gonna push me? You gonna hit me?

KAREEM: Yeah. I fuckin' am. Last warnin', yeah. Get out the fuckin' way.

ALISHA: Fuck off –

KAREEM shoves ALISHA, knocking her to the floor. He hurls himself upon IMAN and starts punching. ALISHA gets back on her feet and, with a roar, charges at, and leaps on top of, KAREEM. When MISS enters, she finds all three students brawling on the floor. For a moment, she stands still, in astonished silence. Then, without a word, she picks up the bin, walks over to the students, and empties the water that has collected in it – a lot of water – on top of them. The students ad-lib cries – 'What the fuck?' 'Oh my god!' 'Fuckin' hell!' 'Bin juice, man!' etc. – but the water has the desired effect. They disentangle themselves from one another. Pause. They remain on the floor, wet, looking up at MISS who is giving them an almighty death stare. Eventually –

MISS: Get up. All of you.

Short pause. No one moves.

MISS: *(Firmer.)* Get up. Now.

They all stand up. They face MISS, shrinking beneath the ferocity of her glare.

MISS: What. The hell. Is going on?

KAREEM: He stole the recorders, miss.

MISS: …Excuse me?

KAREEM: Iman stole the recorders. They're right here in his bag, see.

MISS examines the contents of the bag. A moment passes. The students are all waiting to see how she will respond to this revelation. Beat. MISS takes one of the recorders out of the bag and puts the bag down –

MISS: Sit down. We're doing the assessment.

KAREEM: …What?

MISS: All of you, take a seat. We are doing the speaking and listening assessment.

ALISHA: Miss, we're kinda wet –

MISS: I don't care –

KAREEM: He stole the recorders.

MISS: I can see that, Kareem.

KAREEM: What you gonna do about it?

MISS: I am going to record your assessment.

KAREEM: Fuck's sake, man. He deleted my work. He deleted my coursework. Now he stole the recorders. He been tryin' to fuck me up since the start and you ain't done nothin' about it –

MISS: WE ARE DOING THE ASSESSMENT, DO YOU HEAR ME?

ALISHA: Miss, you're shoutin' bare loud.

MISS: I AM NOT SHOUTING BARE LOUD. YOU WILL KNOW WHEN I AM SHOUTING BARE LOUD, OKAY…? THIS IS ME SHOUTING BARE LOUD. CAN YOU TELL THE DIFFERENCE? THIS IS SHOUTING BARE LOUD!!!

Stunned silence. MISS is wild-eyed, breathing heavily. The students are scared, genuinely scared. After a short pause –

MISS: CAN YOU HEAR ME, CAN YOU…? CAN YOU SEE ME…? THIS IS MY LIFE…IT'S MY FUCKING LIFE…THIS…LOOK…THIS TATTY FUCKING STUPID EXERCISE BOOK FILLED WITH INANE, INDECIPHERABLE, WITLESS SHIT. THAT'S MY LIFE. SAVAGES MAULING ONE ANOTHER ON THE FLOOR. THAT IS MY LIFE. THAT'S WHO I AM…FUCK!!!

More silence. The students are mortified. After another pause –

KAREEM: You shouldn't swear at us, miss –

MISS: What did you say?

KAREEM: …Nothing.

Beat.

MISS: Sit down. Now. Alisha and Kareem, you're doing the assessment. Iman, get on with your coursework.

Short pause. No one moves.

MISS: Do it!

IMAN slinks back to his seat.

KAREEM: Miss, where should we…?

MISS: Jesus Christ –

MISS very forcefully grabs two chairs and a desk and arranges them for the assessment. She thrusts out her hands as if to say, 'There! Sit there!' KAREEM and ALISHA sit down. They look at MISS, not quite sure what to do now. A drop of water lands on their desk. They're sitting under the leak. KAREEM and ALISHA look up at the ceiling –

KAREEM: Aw, the leak…

KAREEM and ALISHA look at each other –

KAREEM: …Eh, left a bit –

MISS closes her eyes, entering a place beyond exasperation, while KAREEM and ALISHA awkwardly shuffle the chairs and the desk out of the way of the leak.

KAREEM: Nah, nah, the other left, the other left –

They move the other way. They stop. They look up at the ceiling again.

KAREEM: I think that's –

ALISHA: Yeah.

KAREEM: Yeah.

Short pause.

MISS: *(Opens eyes.)* Okay –

KAREEM: Miss, my boxers is bare wet though.

MISS: I do not care.

MISS places the audio recorder on the desk in front of KAREEM and ALISHA.

MISS: Right. Ready?

KAREEM: …Eh, I need my notes.

MISS steams over to the desk KAREEM was sitting at earlier, violently grabs the notes, and thrusts them at KAREEM.

KAREEM: Thanks.

ALISHA: Miss, me too, I need my –

MISS fetches ALISHA's notebook and thrusts it at her.

ALISHA: Thank you.

MISS: Now. Are we ready?

KAREEM: *(Thinly veiled sarcasm.)* Sure.

MISS presses 'Record' on the device, but then realises –

MISS: *(Barely audible.)* I haven't got the fucking… *(From memory, she recites somewhat haltingly.)* Green Hill High School. Centre number…137…67. Cambridge IGCSE. First Language English, 0522. Component…6, speaking and listening. Examiner: Mrs – *(Corrects herself.)* Miss Murphy. Date: October…12th 2016. First speaker, candidate name…

ALISHA: Alisha Soneji.

MISS: Candidate number…

ALISHA: …Two-zero-five-seven.

MISS: Second speaker, candidate name…

KAREEM: Kareem Tamam.

MISS: Candidate number…

KAREEM: Two-nine-seven-six.

MISS gestures for them to begin the assessment. She takes a seat at one of the student desks.

ALISHA: *(Flat and awkward.)* Hello and welcome to Room 101…Our first guest this evenin' is Kareem Tamam. Let's have a big round of applause for Kareem.

ALISHA pauses, waits for the imaginary audience to applaud, but of course there's only silence. IMAN turns around briefly, half-checking to see if there is an audience.

ALISHA: So, Kareem, tell us about your first item.

KAREEM: …Eh, thank you, Alisha. My first item is…liars… People who lie. Eh…

KAREEM hesitates. He has noticed MISS. She's not taking notes or even paying attention. She is slumped forward, eyes closed, head in hands.

KAREEM: The thing about liars, yeah…The thing…about liars… *(Breaks off.)* Miss, ain't you meant to like listen? Take notes and stuff.

Short pause. MISS doesn't respond. KAREEM looks at ALISHA: 'What do we do?'

ALISHA: Miss, are you okay?

After a pause, MISS stands up abruptly –

MISS: Kareem, Alisha, I need you to leave.

KAREEM and ALISHA look at each other and then at MISS – they're confused.

MISS: We'll do this tomorrow, okay. I'll come find you… sometime. Iman, I want to talk to you now.

KAREEM: Miss, like –

MISS: I'll find you tomorrow, alright, Kareem. We'll sort it all out…For now, just – I need you to…

No one moves.

MISS: Go! Get out! / Go on!

KAREEM: Alright…Jeez, man.

ALISHA and KAREEM exit, shaking their heads. IMAN remains seated. After a long pause –

MISS: Why did you take the recorders?

IMAN: …

MISS: I asked you a question: why did you take the audio recorders?

IMAN: …

MISS: Iman, I am this close to calling the police. Not only did you deliberately disrupt an official GCSE assessment, you tried to steal school property – expensive equipment. I want to know why.

Short pause.

IMAN: I don't know why…I'm tired of being bullied, I guess.

MISS: …You're tired of being bullied…? By who…? By Kareem…? Is that…?

IMAN nods.

MISS: …How? How does Kareem bully you?

IMAN: …

MISS: Iman, what does he / do –

IMAN: He puts me down. He says nasty things about me and my family. He's been doing it for five years. He's been getting away with it for five years.

MISS: …Okay, so that's…So you thought…You thought you'd get him back…by stealing the *(trails off, unable to finish the sentence)* …That just doesn't make any sense.

Beat.

MISS: Did you delete his story?

IMAN: …

MISS: Did you?

IMAN: …Yes.

Short pause.

MISS: Why?

IMAN: I just told you why. It wasn't even his story though.

MISS: …What?

IMAN: It was Alisha's story.

MISS: …

IMAN: Alisha wrote it, miss. She wrote Kareem's story. That's why it was good.

MISS: …No, she didn't. Kareem wrote the story.

IMAN: Not all of it. Most of it was Alisha. I saw her. It was the day you were late.

MISS: …You saw…Alisha writing the story?

IMAN: Yes. I saw – Alisha was telling Kareem what to write. What words to use. She was typing the words.

Short pause – MISS shakes her head or makes some other gesture of disbelief before –

MISS: Just that one story, or…?

IMAN: Probably all of his coursework, but I didn't – I only saw…that one.

Short pause.

IMAN: Is Alisha in trouble?

Short pause.

MISS: I don't know.

Short pause.

IMAN: Am I in trouble?

Beat.

IMAN: You can't tell on me. Because I could tell on you.

MISS: I'm sorry, what?

IMAN: You swore at us. You threw water at us…You're not supposed to do that.

MISS: …You need to leave now, Iman –

IMAN: You could get in a lot of trouble –

MISS: Leave –

IMAN: You could lose your job.

Short pause.

IMAN: I could make you lose your job.

JOHN enters. After a short, uncomfortable pause –

JOHN: Iman, I need a word with miss –

IMAN: I was leaving anyway, sir.

IMAN looks at MISS. She gives him a nod.

IMAN: Thanks, miss. Sir.

IMAN goes.

MISS: John, how / are you –

JOHN: Did you throw a bucket of water on the Year 12s?

MISS: …

JOHN: I just saw Kareem and Alisha outside. Angry and…
wet! Saying you threw a fuckin' bucket of water on 'em.
You were shoutin' at 'em. Swearin'.

MISS: …

JOHN: Is that true?

MISS: …No.

JOHN: No…?

Short pause.

MISS: It wasn't a bucket. It was a bin.

JOHN: …What…?

MISS: It was a bin full of water. Not a bucket –

JOHN: What the fuck!?! What difference does it make it was a fuckin' bin!?! You can't do that! You can't throw a fuckin', a fuckin' *receptacle* of water on the students!

MISS: I know. I'm sorry –

JOHN: Jesus! Why!?! Why would you do that!?!

MISS: …There was a fight, okay. They were fighting. The three of them. On the floor. On top of each other. Like animals…I poured some water on them. That's all. I stopped the fight.

JOHN: …Okay. Alright. So you…Okay. You stopped the fight?

MISS: Yes.

JOHN: Right. Good. Now we're – Good. So you were – health and safety! You were protectin' the students.

MISS: Exactly.

JOHN: Okay. Yes. You were safeguardin' the welfare of the students. You were doin' your job.

MISS: Yes!

JOHN: Christ Almighty. *(Sighs.)* Did you swear at them?

MISS: …No.

JOHN: You didn't?

MISS: No. I mean, it was – they were fighting. I was firm –

JOHN: Okay, but that's not – there's a difference between firm and –

MISS: I can tell the difference, John. I know what swearing is –

JOHN: No, obviously, but why then – why would they –

MISS: John…I didn't swear…I did not swear…

Short pause.

JOHN: You're sure?

MISS: Yes.

JOHN: Iman will corroborate that?

MISS: …Absolutely…Speak to Iman. He'll tell you…

JOHN: *(Shakes his head.)* …It's fine. I believe you. Look, are you okay here?

MISS: Yes!

JOHN: …You're holding it together?

MISS: Yes! There was a fight, John. Fights happen in schools. I dealt with it. I'm holding it together.

JOHN: Alright. Sorry…I'm sorry…

MISS: I'm perfectly in control here.

JOHN: Good…Right. All I want to hear…Listen, I need to call Mr Tamam. And the other parents. Sort this out. I'll speak to you later.

JOHN goes to leave.

MISS: John.

He stops.

JOHN: Yes.

Beat.

MISS: Saturday night – Rachel's with James…

Short pause.

JOHN: I don't…I'm not…

MISS: You could take me out…

Pause.

JOHN: I already have plans.

Short pause.

MISS: What plans?

JOHN: …Plans.

MISS: Cancel them.

JOHN: …I can't.

MISS: You can't cancel your plans? For me?

JOHN: …No.

MISS: …Oh…Okay…

Short, awkward pause.

MISS: We could do something now?

JOHN: …What do you mean?

MISS: I could use a good ride.

JOHN: …Excuse me?

MISS: We could have a shag.

JOHN: …What…? Now? Here?

MISS: Yes.

JOHN: I'm SLT! I can't have sex in a classroom! Jesus –

MISS: Okay. I was only asking –

JOHN: What the fuck –

MISS: I thought you wanted to – I thought you wanted *me* –

JOHN: I do. I *did*.

Short pause.

MISS: …You *did*…? Past tense…?

Pause.

JOHN: I was with someone else.

MISS: …Hah?

JOHN: At the weekend. I slept with someone else.

MISS: …You…? Oh…Who…?

JOHN: …

MISS: Someone from school?

JOHN: …You said – You told me –

MISS: I told you I needed some time.

JOHN: It's been almost a year.

Short pause.

JOHN: I'm sorry…I didn't intend…It just sort of happened.

MISS: No, it's…

Short pause.

MISS: Is that your 'plans'? Your Saturday night?

JOHN nods. After a short pause –

MISS: So it's like a – it's a thing now –

JOHN: Don't do that –

MISS: It's not just a one-off –

JOHN: Please.

Short pause.

MISS: Who is it?

JOHN: …

MISS: Come on. Just tell me who it is.

JOHN: I can't –

MISS: Not like in a weird way –

JOHN: I'm not gonna tell you, okay. It wouldn't be right.

Short pause.

MISS: I'll be wondering. I'll be walking down the corridors, picturing you naked with like every female teacher I pass.

JOHN: Right, well, that does sound a little weird actually.

Short pause.

JOHN: It's not a one-off thing. I mean…I don't know…I like her.

MISS: Oh…

Short pause.

JOHN: Sorry.

MISS: No. I'm happy for you, John. Congratulations.

JOHN: It ain't exactly marriage or anything. We've had like one drunken…never mind…Thank you though. For understanding.

MISS: You're welcome…Sorry for the…borderline sexual harassment.

JOHN: That's okay.

Short pause.

JOHN: I better go make these calls.

MISS: Yep.

JOHN: I'll see you.

MISS: See you.

Short pause.

JOHN: Are you okay?

MISS: Yes. I'm fine.

JOHN: Good.

JOHN leaves.

MISS: I'm fine…Every day I make greatness happen.

Blackout.

SCENE FOURTEEN

About three months later: the end of January, 2017.

The room is empty. After a moment, IMAN's first entrance from the beginning of the play is re-enacted almost identically: we hear a knock on the door. A few seconds later, the door opens tentatively, and IMAN sticks his head in. He looks around then enters, sits down, opens his bag, looks inside, but then he stops – he doesn't remove his pencil case or set out his things. He only slumps in his chair.

After a pause, MISS enters. Again, we are reminded of her first entrance. Papers, folders, a teacher's planner, and a laptop spill from her arms – but she too is different: less frantic.

MISS: Hi Iman.

IMAN nods. MISS puts her stuff down.

MISS: You okay?

IMAN: *(Sarcasm.)* Great.

MISS smiles at him sympathetically. After a short pause –

MISS: Well…why don't we get to work?

IMAN: Aren't you going to give me a big speech about how I only have one shot and all the rest of it?

Short pause.

MISS: Look, I'm sorry about the result, Iman. I know you don't want to be here. But what can we do? We just keep trying…Let's take a look at your folder, shall we?

IMAN: What's the point?

MISS: …You need to pass GCSE English. That's the point –

IMAN: I'm not going to pass. I'm going to fail. Again. For the third time. I'm a failure. That's who I am. That's what I do.

MISS: You're not a failure…You're still here. You're still fighting. We both are. Come on. This time we'll make sure you pass.

IMAN looks at her a moment, then –

IMAN: *(Gets up.)* I need the toilet.

IMAN goes out. MISS drops her mask. She exhales, closes her eyes, perhaps massages her own forehead with her fingers. A drop of water falls from the ceiling. Beat. She opens her eyes. She looks up at the ceiling. She climbs up onto one of the desks. She reaches out. She touches the ceiling. Part of it crumbles, comes away in her hand. She drops it on the floor. She reaches out for the ceiling again, this time applying more force when she touches it. A torrent of water is unleashed. It gushes down all over her – soaking her hair, her face, her clothes, her body – and she lets it happen. She stands still beneath it, eyes closed, allowing herself to be drenched.

IMAN returns.

IMAN: *(As he enters.)* Okay. I'm ready –

He stops. He looks at her. She doesn't seem to have registered his entrance.

IMAN: Uh, miss, the ceiling is leaking…

A second deluge bursts forth, this time soaking IMAN. Like MISS, he stands still – he lets it happen. Eventually, both leaks subside. For a time, MISS and IMAN stay where they are, sodden and unmoving.

IMAN: Well, this is a pretty fucking depressing situation…

After a pause, IMAN moves forward so he can see MISS's face.

IMAN: Miss…

Her eyes are open now, brimming with tears.

IMAN: Are you okay…? Maybe you should come down from there.

He offers her his hand. She takes it. He helps her down off the desk and into a seat. He's not really sure what to do or say. He sits down too. After a pause –

IMAN: I'm sorry I threatened to get you fired.

MISS makes a barely perceptible nod of acknowledgement. After another pause –

IMAN: Do you like Woody Allen?

MISS: …What?

IMAN: Woody Allen. You mentioned him. Ages ago…Eighty per cent of success is showing up.

MISS: Oh. Right…Actually, yes. I do. I love Woody Allen.

IMAN: You do?!?

MISS: Yes.

IMAN: So do I!

Short, weird pause.

MISS: Okay.

Another short, weird pause.

MISS: You're pretty weird, Iman.

IMAN: …I know…So are you.

MISS: Yeah. Fair enough.

Short pause.

IMAN: What's the other twenty per cent?

MISS: I don't know, Iman. I don't know. *(Gets up, grabs a laptop from the teacher's desk.)* Come on. Let's – We should get started –

IMAN: Don't you want to dry off?

MISS: No. I'm fine. Are you alright?

IMAN: Uh, I guess.

MISS: Okay. Good. Look, let's forget the folder. Forget everything else. Just…type what I say.

IMAN: …What?

MISS: Let me dictate to you. Let me tell you what to write.

IMAN: …Miss, that's cheating.

Beat.

IMAN: Are you sure…?

MISS: …No, but…

IMAN: …Okay.

MISS: Right. Ready?

IMAN nods. As MISS speaks, IMAN starts to type her words, and the lights begin to fade slowly.

MISS: *(Slowly.)* 'Dear Samantha Brick…I am writing to you… in response to your…outrageous article…published in… the *Daily Mail…*'

Short pause.

MISS: '…Frankly, you should be ashamed of yourself…'

Short pause.

MISS: '…Your article is a pathetic web of inconsistencies, contradictions and lies –'

Blackout.

END OF PLAY

Printed in the USA
CPSIA information can be obtained
at www.ICGtesting.com
LVHW020846171024
794056LV00002B/429